THAT GIRL IN YOUR MIRROR

Vonda Kay Van Dyke

That
Girl
in Your Mirror

FLEMING H. REVELL COMPANY
WESTWOOD, NEW JERSEY

Acknowledgments

A special thank-you to Phyllis Murphy for her help, and also to Fleming H. Revell Company for their consideration and efforts.

Cover photograph by Robert Dykstra

With love
to my mother and father

❧ Preface

There is a stairway to beauty that presents an enormous challenge to every young girl and it takes work, patience, and time to climb.

Each step to beauty will be hard to mount alone in the dark, but with God's light and His guiding hand, you'll find your way to new heights of beauty.

When you think you've reached the top of the stairs, take a long look at that girl in your mirror. You'll see that she has a new air of beauty about her. She'll show a wider, more confident smile, and she'll possess that inner sparkle that only Christ can give.

But don't primp and admire too long, because if you let your gaze wander past your reflection you'll discover that you are merely standing on the landing of another stairway that extends farther than your sight and longer than your life.

Contents

THAT GIRL IN YOUR MIRROR

1

Who Are You, Really?

❀ *I got the*
jolt of my life when a seventeen-year-old girl asked me
whether things had changed much since I was a teen-ager. I
was only twenty-one at the time!

The question came during a press conference at the beginning of my year as Miss America, and it left me a little breath-
less. It was soon to be repeated, however, and very often—just
about every time my plane touched ground, which was almost
every day.

I had been like any other girl when I turned twenty. I felt it
was quite an accomplishment and expected all kinds of important changes to take place in my life. Of course, I never
dreamed that a teen-ager would begin to look upon me as someone in another generation!

But that's how the teens are, I guess. They begin abruptly
and end suddenly, which is awfully hard on the young people
who have to make the adjustments. One day you're a child of
twelve—a matter of two-plus-two equals four, as far as everyone else is concerned—and the next morning, on your thir-
teenth birthday, you're a teen-ager—someone mysterious, un-
predictable, complicated, and oh-so-touchy.

If you really work at it for the next seven years, you might
begin to learn what the teens are all about—and whoosh!
another birthday comes along and rockets you into your twen-

ties! Those years have their problems, too, although you never hear much about them.

So it's no wonder young people have a lot of questions on their minds. Youth is worse than Mark Twain's definition of the weather—everybody talks about it, but in this case nobody seems to know what it means.

I began to realize that this was why so many young girls came to my press conferences. It gave them an opportunity to ask a lot of questions, not only of me but of themselves. They were the ones who were really on the spot.

Whenever I saw teen-agers—boys as well as girls—among the reporters at an airport, I knew that my brains were going to get a real workout. But I looked forward to it. Those kids wanted straight answers, and if they didn't agree with what I said, they let me know it. They taught me to think very carefully before I spoke.

I certainly don't claim to be an authority on girls and the things on their minds. I can only speak as one of them to all of them. And even though I've passed ahead into my twenties, I can still manage to look "way back thar" to the days when I was in my teens. I loved those years, every minute of them, and I thank God for helping me to make them a strong foundation for the rest of my life.

It's no joke—there *is* a world of difference between nineteen and twenty! When you're twenty, you're supposed to know what life is all about. Don't ask me how—it's just supposed to happen! Even if you don't know all the answers, people think you do, and this in itself is a pretty comfortable feeling. But teen-agers don't usually get that kind of break. They're supposed to be mixed-up, panicky, lost, and no one even gives them the credit for knowing some of the questions.

I know better, not only from my own experience as a teen-ager, but from the talks I've had with young people. Yes, things have changed since I was a teen-ager—in spite of all the problems, things have improved!

I won't deny that lots of girls in their teens and twenties are

14

still confused. They don't quite know what to make of themselves, of their future, of the world around them. But they're not taking everything for granted—they want to know how? why? why not? And they're entitled to the answers!

"How will you learn if you don't ask?" is something we've heard since childhood. It's good advice, too, although it doesn't go far enough. Yes, a girl should ask questions—ask your parents, your teachers, your minister, your friends, me, anyone in the world—but be sure to ask yourself. Qualified or not, you're the specialist in the subject of you.

Most people are flattered when someone comes to them for advice, and I'm no exception. I could talk to the girls for hours —and I do, whenever I have the opportunity—but I realize that my opinions, my experiences with specific problems, can supply only part of the answers they need. The other part can be found in themselves. This is something I didn't always have time to explain when I was running to catch a plane, and I want to make it perfectly clear now.

You can ask me any question, and I'll do my best to answer it, straight from the shoulder, but I'm not laying down a law when I give an opinion. I can only give you my point of view, based on what was good for me, and that's something you'll have to evaluate for yourself. Hold my answer up to the light, look at it from all sides, see how it stands up. In other words, cut yourself in on the act.

Too often young people give all their attention to other people—usually their idols—and they are generous to a fault. They can be the most devoted, dedicated people in the world when it comes to someone else, but when they try to concentrate on themselves, their thoughts go off in all directions. Of course they feel confused!

Every girl deserves a fair share of her own attention, and that involves concentration, not conceit. God gave you a mind and He expects you to use it—now! But if you're going to fall for that propaganda about the young years being a waste of time, or a "stage" you simply have to suffer through, then concentration is not for you. It takes practice and determination.

Now is *not* the time to take a break from living, growing, and making something of yourself. These are the truly workable years, the years that can set the pattern for your future, and it's a shame to squander them by playing a waiting game. What are you waiting for, anyway? Maturity? What's that? Maturity doesn't drop into your lap at a certain age—you have to grow into it, slowly, with your eyes wide open every inch of the way. And the funny thing about it is that when you stop worrying about becoming mature, that's when you discover that you've made it.

I won't say that these young years are the best years of your life—I couldn't stand it when someone said that to me. It reminds me of the people who warned Columbus not to set sail for India because the earth was flat and he might fall off the edge of it. Well, what are we supposed to do when we come to the end of our youth?—fall off the edge of life? I will say that these years ought to be the busiest ones, because you've got work to do! If you want to be something, or someone, up ahead in that future of yours, you'd better get started now. Achievement takes more than a snap of the fingers and a big fat wish. It takes discovery, practice, and daring.

First, you have to discover the real you, which isn't a simple matter. Not only do you have to learn how you tick, but how you can tick best. Everybody can do something, and you're no different from the rest of us, but maybe you can improve on the way you do it. This takes a lot of digging, which is another way of saying that you can't get by on talent alone. Finally, you'll never know how high you can go in the world if you keep staring at the ground. Here's where you have to be daring.

Most of the teen-aged girls I've known look forward to becoming adults, but they don't want to skip their youth to do it. And why should they? They know those years are good for something, even if they aren't quite sure what to do with them. Yes, they can have fun for a while, living from one exciting moment to the next, but sooner or later they'll want to get off that merry-go-round of giggles. They don't want the future to slam into them someday when they're not looking. They want to get ready for it.

How can you do that? How can you get a glimpse of the future you? There's only one way, the best way—get to know the present you, the girl you really are and always will be.

When you think about it, there isn't any other way to get ready for your future. It isn't something that exists outside you. Your future is in you, at this very moment. It depends upon you—upon your understanding of yourself and the way you make use of your abilities. Who else can do it for you?

If you feel you're too young to discover what kind of a person you are, stop and think a moment. You're old enough to know right from wrong, even if you don't always make the best choice between them. You get that creepy feeling when you've done the wrong thing, don't you? Then you *do* know.

You're also old enough to set your mind on something, but why does your target always have to be something like a new dress or a car. You've got a lot on the ball—why not use it for more important things?

God has given you opportunities, and faith can open your eyes to them, but you have to do your part, too! You could get the best breaks in the world, every day of your life, and they wouldn't do a thing for you as long as you just sat there, staring into space. Life can't make something out of you. You have to make something out of your life.

I've been in a number of beauty pageants, and I've watched a good many more as Miss America, and I've seen a lot of beautiful girls lose to someone whose features were less than perfect. There's a reason for it. Sometimes the girl who is blessed with flawless physical beauty finds it a handicap because she begins to count on it too much. But the girl who realizes that her nose is a bit too short, or her eyes are too far apart, begins to pay more attention to her personality. As she becomes more objective about herself, she gradually learns all there is to know about herself. Then she goes to work correcting those faults, boosting her merits, trying, practicing, improving herself until she becomes a truly outstanding girl. No, she doesn't win the judges' vote by accident—she earns it!

Maybe you're a fairly critical girl who doesn't have a very high opinion of herself. Well, get ready to go to work on yourself! The girl who trusts to a pretty face or a sensational figure or an expensive wardrobe may seem to be far ahead of you, but believe me, she's the turtle and you're about to take off like a bunny!

2

Who Would You Like to Be?

❦ *Your best friend*

may be a stunning girl, but don't try to look exactly like her! That girl on the magazine cover may have a cute hairstyle, but think carefully before you cut your hair as short as hers.

Are you changing the slant of your handwriting? Are you trying to force a husky quality into your voice? Where on earth did you get that southern accent? You're supposed to be discovering the real you—why are you running off in so many different directions?

Most of us find it much easier to copy someone we admire, especially someone who has already "made it." It seems like a surefire formula, doesn't it? If the most popular girl in school wears long bangs and slouches against the nearest wall while she talks to the boys who constantly surround her, why not copy her style? Why not?

Well, for one thing, you might look terrible in bangs. And you're a little short-waisted, so you should always stand as straight as you can. You'd better look for another formula. But where? The girl on the magazine cover has a face something like yours—almost, anyway. Of course, you can see only her head in the photograph, and you can't be sure how tall she is. Her height could have influenced her taste in hairstyles, couldn't it?

Appearances and clothes aren't the only things you're tempted to imitate. Sometimes you try to make yourself think

19

the way someone else does—or the way you think she thinks. It isn't very comfortable, is it? It can make you stop thinking altogether.

There's a look that's right for you. There are thoughts that only you can think, principles only you can fashion. There is such a thing as your own particular style of doing things. These are the things that will identify you to others, the things that will find you a permanent place in people's minds and hearts, if only you can find them in yourself first.

Don't be discouraged if all the things you admire seem to be in other people. You may be able to find the same qualities in yourself, and you may even find some that are better.

Go ahead and admire people. It's good for you. It will make you more objective about yourself and more willing to make some improvements. Just don't go so far in your admiration that you get lost in someone else's personality. That's what James Boswell did by living so many years in the shadow of Dr. Samuel Johnson. He gave us a brilliant biography of that remarkable man, but his own personality remains a mystery.

Let your admiration inspire you to attempt the things you see other girls achieving. It's a good way to try out your talents. Of course, you won't discover anything worthwhile unless you admire someone outstanding, so be a little choosy about the women you imitate.

I'll always be grateful to the women who set good examples for me when I was growing up. I never would have attempted some of the things I did if it hadn't been for them. I owe a debt of thanks to a dean of women who had an amazing gift for public speaking. I was always a ham, the kind of girl who thrived on school plays and class programs, but I had never given careful thought to the way I spoke when I wasn't playing a part. When I heard how beautifully the dean of women could communicate an idea, I realized how important it was to speak clearly at all times. I began to practice.

I don't even remember the name of the girl who encouraged me to walk with a lighter step. I saw her at a beauty pageant when she floated down the ramp as if there were nothing but air beneath her feet, and I'll never forget how I suddenly understood the meaning of gracefulness.

My mother is a very determined woman, and I think a little determination rubbed off on me because I admired it in her—and I still do. If my mother sets her mind on something, you can be sure she'll achieve it, no matter how long it takes. When she and my father were married, she had to interrupt her education, but that didn't mean she abandoned it. No, indeed! During my sophomore year in college, my mother was also a student on the same campus, and she got her degree ahead of me!

No, I don't see anything wrong with admiration if it isn't overdone. It gets you started down the road to self-discovery, but that's as far as it goes. You have to go on alone.

You'll be in new territory, and you'll have to learn to be very objective about yourself. It won't do to select your favorite characteristics and try to make do with them. You may not have the best judgment, you know, and some of the features you reject may really be valuable.

You shouldn't attempt to be analytical about yourself unless you have some self-respect, or at least a willingness to acquire it, because you have to be able to stand up under a lot of constructive criticism. If you don't have enough self-respect, you'll simply wilt under your own critical appraisal.

Most teen-aged girls are extremely self-critical, but, judging from some of the questions they have asked me, I'd say that their criticism is far from constructive. I've never known any group of people who ran themselves down so much! There's a big difference between the kind of criticism that tears a girl apart and leaves her in pieces and the kind that looks for a weak spot in order to strengthen it.

If you met a new girl in your school, you'd give her a chance to demonstrate the kind of person she was—or at least I hope you would! Well, you deserve the same break. You're being much too hard on yourself if you're trying to be like someone

21

else—that's an impossible demand. No matter what you see in others and what you don't see in yourself, you can't swap, and when you can accept that fact, you'll be ready for another important discovery: we're all a mixture of good and bad features and characteristics, with a lot of mediocre qualities thrown in. The girl you admire may think she has a lot of shortcomings that you couldn't begin to see because she has learned how to make the most of her assets. This is what you can learn to do, once you've taken your inventory.

The most successful girl in the world is the girl who can be herself. Once you make up your mind that you're going to be you, you're in for a great adventure, and the discoveries will never end. You may get to know yourself pretty well right now, but think how much you're going to change as the years go by. In fact, you'll be able to choose some of those changes!

3

It Takes Courage
to Be Yourself

❧ *Some girls make*

a big fuss over their individuality, and in a way you can't blame
them. It's quite thrilling to realize that you're distinctly different from everyone else you know. But before you season your
conversation with too much "I," you had better stop and remember that you discovered something that's been there all
the time.

That's right—from the day you were born you've been an
individual. Your baby cries were not the same as any other
baby's, and your view of the world through the bars of your
crib was your very own. You learned to move around, to talk,
to behave, to play, and to read—all in your own time and your
own style. You received all the world's wonderful gifts in a
unique way.

Now the time has come for you to start putting things back
into the world, and no one else will do it in quite the same
way. You can put things back into the world by expressing
yourself, your individuality, to others—this is the real meaning
of being yourself.

Now you know why it is so important for you to understand what kind of a person you are. You can hardly express
someone else's personality, can you?

You can't be yourself by going off in a corner, either. That's not the way to express your individuality, but it's a good way to lose it! You can't function as a whole person unless you mix it up with people, lots of people. A personality isn't much good unless it is used and developed, and you won't learn anything about yours until you try it out on other people.

Are you afraid that you'll lose your precious individuality if you become one of the crowd? You may have a point there. It's hard to be yourself and please the crowd at the same time, but it might help you if you remember that you don't have to please the whole crowd all of the time.

It takes individual people to make up any group, or any gang, or any crowd, and they don't necessarily surrender their individuality by getting together. At least, they don't *have to* give it up, although some girls seem to be eager to do it.

If the crowd insists that you smother your own personality and go along with everyone else, then that's not the crowd for you. It doesn't matter if it's the "in" crowd—it won't last long. Any group needs the personality of each member or it has none of its own. Conformity is colorless, so go and find the crowd that will welcome you for what you are.

Be careful, though, that you don't go too far in the other direction. You don't have to conform, but you should try to be agreeable. Don't be the girl who is so obsessed with her individuality that she refuses to do what anyone else wants to do. She's not herself—she's a pest!

Even though you may have your ups and downs, the experience of being in a group will be good for you. Individuals have to learn to respect each other's wishes if they want to get things done, and a little difference of opinion won't hurt them.

Don't be afraid to be different. Sometimes you can express yourself in only one way, a way no one has ever tried. It isn't wrong just because it's new; it's wrong if it will hurt someone, and this is something you would have to consider no matter how you wanted to express yourself.

Some girls will tell you to go ahead and be different—if you've got the nerve. They seem to think people will stare, or boo, or ridicule you if you don't do things in the same old way. But they don't know much about people!

For some reason, I've been doing things differently since I was a little girl. When I was in high school I had the double distinction of being the only girl in the printing class and the only girl who had ever played the tenor saxophone in the school band. I didn't do any of these things simply to be different, but I didn't see why my interest in printing or my enjoyment of the tenor sax should be choked off because I was a girl. And no one poked fun at me—not the school principal, not the boys in the print shop, not the other members of the band. In fact, they seemed to think I had made the most natural choices in the world.

Life holds out so many wonderful opportunities to each of us that it's a shame to say "no" to some of them simply because we're girls. If you think women were created just to sit and spin, open your Bible to the stories of Esther, Naomi, Deborah, Priscilla, and Mary. Imagine how much the world would have lost if they had said, "Oh, I can't do that—no woman has ever done anything like that!" when God called them.

I don't know why more girls haven't become ventriloquists, although I must admit I was first attracted to it because it was so unusual. I used to watch Paul Winchell and his dummy Jerry Mahoney on television when I was about six years old, and the idea of one man holding a conversation with himself caught hold of my imagination. It certainly wasn't something that everybody else was doing!

As my interest grew I began to practice until I could "throw" my voice so that it seemed to come from another part of the room. I remember how I used to sit at the dinner table and ask my father to "please pass the butter" in a voice that seemed to come from behind him. He would ask me to do it again for my mother, and then we would all laugh.

When my parents saw that I kept working on my technique, they gave me a small Jerry Mahoney dummy for my seventh birthday. What a day that was! For once, I could hardly think of anything to say when I opened that long box and looked in to find that red-haired, wide-mouthed, saucer-eyed, funny little doll lying among the layers of tissue paper. He was only a piece of wood in snappy clothes, and when I took him out of the box and held him on my lap he would have fallen in a heap on the floor if I hadn't held him up. Slowly I began to poke around the mechanisms on his back until I found out how to make his mouth open and close. It would take a lot of practice to synchronize the mouth openings with the words he would seem to speak, but already I could see my little dummy taking on a sparkle of life.

I couldn't wait, and I began to hold a conversation with the little fellow. It was clumsy and I didn't give him the same voice all the time, but right before my eyes that piece of wood took on a personality! He wasn't limp and lifeless any more— he seemed to be in constant motion! He looked over his shoulder, drew his head back in surprise, shook his head. I never had such a good time!

Ventriloquism has always been a lot of fun for me. Of course, being a girl ventriloquist at the age of seven was certainly different, but I enjoyed the novelty of it and my friends took it in stride. I was simply the girl with the dummy—I had my hobby and my friends had theirs. That's the way friends should be, and you should be able to relax with them.

It's almost impossible to relax with a crowd and I hope you won't let this discourage you. One of the biggest obstacles to being yourself is your own worry that people won't like you when they get to know you. Sometimes, in an effort to become popular, a girl will abandon her own convictions and follow the will of the crowd because she thinks that is the only way to please people. Well, maybe it is—and where does that leave her? For the moment, she rates with the crowd, but where does she stand in her own opinion?

What you think of yourself is very important. Don't expect to be able to please everyone you meet, but always try to live up to the standards you set for yourself. If you are ever faced

26

with choosing between your own self-approval and the approval of someone else, don't get cold feet. Stick to your principles! You can live with someone else's frown, but you'll be miserable with your own.

If you have been completely honest with yourself, you'll know when you're about to do something that isn't right for you. You can often cover up with other people, but don't try to fool yourself. You can't make yourself believe you're something other than what you are.

I'll make you a promise. If you will take a deep breath and try to be your own genuine self for a few days—and then a few weeks—you'll wonder why you were ever afraid to do it. You'll be surprised to find how many people will welcome your fresh and candid personality, and you'll have a far better opinion of yourself.

Once you feel the warmth of people's friendliness, you'll want to be sure you're worthy of it. No matter how much progress you've made, you'll see areas that could use some improvement. After all, the girl you express to others should be the best possible girl you can make of her!

Now you're really getting somewhere. You know who you are and you've introduced yourself to the world. Well, don't just stand there—do something with yourself!

4

Let's Look at
Your Good Points

❧ *When a girl*

takes her abilities for granted, she begins to think she doesn't have any. I've heard some of the most charming, accomplished young women moan, "I don't have any talent at all!"—and they really believed it!

If you are one of these girls, then somebody ought to put you wise. *There is no such thing as an untalented person.* Do you believe those fairy tales about celebrities, the ones that describe a "born" singer, a "born" teacher, or a "born" painter? There's no such thing as that, either! People are born, but they bring only the raw materials of their talent into the world with them. It takes years of hard work and training to make their talents seem so effortless that they appear to have been born that way.

One of the most charming things about talented people is their self-confidence, and this is a kind of beauty every girl should reflect. If you've ever watched a beauty pageant, you can spot it right away in some of the girls. They have such an advantage over the girls who aren't sure of themselves.

Self-confidence isn't a mystery. It's a feeling of trust in your own abilities, and it develops along with your talent. Try it for yourself and see. Whatever you want to do, do it as well as you can. Whether it's playing the piano, making your clothes, editing the school paper, or even working with a dummy, try putting a little muscle into your efforts. If you're determined not to give up after the first few attempts, you'll begin to feel a small but steady glow of confidence as you become more skillful. And why shouldn't you feel confident? You aren't trusting to luck—you're trusting in your own skills and you know exactly what you can do with them. No longer do you have to take a deep breath and hope you won't make a fool of yourself!

Don't waste your abilities, and above all, don't ignore them. You have them for a reason—use them! You'll get plenty of encouragement. Our modern educational system is designed to help you discover your own talents and give them the best possible training. So there's no excuse for the I-can't-do-anything gal.

Your school can whet your appetite for training, but the amount of dedication and effort you put into developing yourself is strictly up to you. No one can force you to do more than the required amount of studying, no one can grab you by the collar and put you to work doing something useful after school. That's the hard part of being yourself—you have to make the decisions and carry them out as well.

It's really too bad when a girl stops short of doing her very best, and this happens quite often. You may practice on the tennis court until you're no longer embarrassed by your serve, but you shouldn't let it go at that. Why not work on your backhand, your return, and all the other features of the game until you feel absolutely confident about the way you play. No, you may not be good enough to try out for the Davis Cup, but you'll have a wonderful feeling of accomplishment.

I've worked with my dummy for a long, long time, and yet I've never reached the point where I could sit back and say, "Well, I made it." When I was a very young ventriloquist I practiced in front of a mirror until I improved my control over my lip and jaw movements when I spoke. When that became almost second nature, I had to turn my attention to the controls at the back of the dummy. I wasn't a very smooth performer in those days, but after enough practice I could get my dummy into action without even thinking about it.

Anything that doesn't have a challenge to it usually loses my interest after a while, and I eventually began to feel that my dummy had nothing more to teach me. How wrong I was! I had overlooked something that needed a lot of improvement—my act! It literally ate up material and I was becoming aware of repeating myself too often. My audiences were varying as they grew larger, and I couldn't always be sure that they would welcome me with the warmth I felt at a Sunday school performance. Obviously I needed much more material, faster timing, and a kind of wit that was ready to ad-lib at a moment's notice. That kind of challenge was almost too big for me, until my mother said, "You'll never know what you can do until you try, Vonda." What could I lose?

I surprised myself, all right! I had always liked to laugh, but I never knew I had any talent for making other people laugh. I even discovered that I could think better on my feet.

A few years later, when I graduated to a professional dummy with movable eyes and a thick shock of red hair, I was certainly glad I had put so much time into my act. I was so excited about working with a big, complicated dummy that I took him to my next appearance without practicing with him. When I got onstage I almost had to do a monologue because I couldn't find the right button to open his mouth! I guess I went through every quip and joke I had ever used while my fingers fiddled furiously behind my dummy, who seemed to be listening intently to every word I said. We made it through that performance somehow, and I managed to get Kurley's mouth open a few times near the end, but I'll never take such a chance again!

Even during my year as Miss America, when I didn't have much time to prepare for anything, I kept my eyes and ears alert for new material that I might be able to use in the future.

I don't think I'll ever learn all there is to know about ventriloquism—or anything else, for that matter.

Incidentally, you may not have realized it, but getting ready for a date, or for school, or just for shopping takes a certain amount of talent—if you want to look attractive without devoting your whole life to your looks. I had a very good example in my mother. In exactly ten minutes flat, my mother could change from casual clothes to something crisp and smart for dinner—and without keeping my father waiting. Like anything else, it becomes a real talent if you work at it.

Lots of girls have asked me why I became a professional performer and I always say that I did it because my father promised me a puppy. Actually, that's only part of the story, and the puppy was more of a prize than a reason.

In our family, we don't believe in being selfish. We believe that we should be willing to share everything, even our abilities, because everything we have comes from the Lord. When my parents bought me my first dummy, they weren't simply rewarding me for my persistence. They were trying to encourage me to let my friends share the fun of the imaginative chatter that goes on between ventriloquist and dummy. I had built a creative little world of my own, and my parents didn't think I should keep all that space to myself.

I probably would have been content to remain the star of the family living room, but my father was much too smart for me. I had wanted a puppy for a long time, and my father agreed to give me one—*if* I could line up a spot for my dummy and me on a school program. In front of all those kids? Yes, indeed!

Well, I took a big gulp and agreed. After all, he hadn't said which school. I had Sunday school in mind—the class was small and I would be able to sing hymns and tell Bible stories, just as I had been doing at home.

My Sunday-school teacher had more nerve than I did—she agreed to let me perform with my dummy during our next class. I've given many performances since that day, but none that gave me such a feeling of achievement. My father was right: the best part of a talent is sharing it. I got a soft, warm, lovable, little fox terrier, but I had already received my reward.

I've been fortunate. I am an only child, and my parents were extremely interested in the way I grew up, but they never smothered me with their own personalities. In fact, they're very strong-minded people, and they wanted me to grow up to be just as strong-minded—*but in my own way.*

Girls need a lot of encouragement from their parents. They need it even more than boys do, because they tend to hold themselves back a bit and parents can give them that important little push into life. Some people say that parents give too much attention to children these days, but if that's true I think it's a good thing. If a girl gets enough attention at home, she won't try to get it by turning a corner on two wheels of her car.

If your parents take an interest in you, they're giving you something to live up to. You'll feel their pride in you for the rest of your life. Because they care about your life and what you do with it, you'll care, too.

You'll have a harder time trying to make something of yourself if you don't have the blessing of parents who care, but that doesn't mean you have to settle for a mediocre life. You aren't really adrift in this world, not if you look a little beyond your everyday acquaintances. God cares about every big and little thing you do and He has a special interest in your life. If you need a good boost to get you started on your way to becoming a more worthwhile person, He can give it to you.

There's only one danger in developing your talents, and that is the temptation to give too much of your time and attention to one particular skill. I believe that a talented girl can do many things, and most of them well. Try lots of things and don't stick to the same field. If you're a good singer, find out how well you can do on the debating team, and then strike out for something entirely different. Get outdoors for a change.

32

Maybe you'd enjoy riding a horse if you'd only give it a try. Or gardening might be the thing for you—it takes real talent to plant tomatoes so that they'll grow!

Like every other girl, you will discover some limitations. I know a lot of girls who run the other way when a basketball heads in their direction, but they can bake the fanciest, most luscious cakes you ever ate. On the other hand, I've met a few terrific water skiers who would have to live on canned beans if they had to do their own cooking.

If you can cut a figure eight on ice skates with your eyes closed, good for you! Now, how about trying something that doesn't seem so easy. It isn't a good idea to stick to the things you pick up without much effort. Suppose you were able to take only the snap courses in school? You might have a great time, but your mind wouldn't get much of a workout. It's the same with your personality. If you don't try to do some of the things that seem difficult to you, you'll become lop-sided! If you really enjoy teamwork—such as basketball, committees, the Girl Scouts—try your hand at tennis, reporting for the school paper, or volunteer hospital work. If you'd rather work on your own, see if you can't increase your patience by taking part in a group project. Even if you still prefer one type of self-expression to another, you need some balance in your life.

Cleopatra is generally thought to have been a great beauty, yet Shakespeare spoke of "her infinite variety" as the most enduring feature of her personality. Actually, she was rather plain except for her nose, which was large and quite distracting, but she was an extremely versatile woman. She had to march at the head of her army, command her navy, keep accounts of her treasury, entertain visiting VIP's, and hold onto her job as Queen of Egypt. How's that for versatility! It's unfortunate that Cleopatra had such an underdeveloped sense of right and wrong, because her achievements were far beneath the effort and ability she put into them.

Perfecting a talent calls for a lot of self-discipline, and you have to be quite serious about it. Some people think girls are too feather-brained to do it. I disagree, emphatically! Of course, I'm partial, but that's not the only reason. I've seen what young girls can do.

You won't ever have a better chance to improve yourself than during your teens and early twenties. Your capabilities are there, just itching to be used. Yes, you can put it off—until you're ninety-six, if you wish. But you'll find it so much easier when you're sixteen!

5

What About Those Faults?

❀ *Are you touchy*

about criticism? You shouldn't be, not if you really want to get
the kinks out of your personality. Unless you're a most ex-
ceptional girl, you've got a blind spot when it comes to your
faults, and criticism can give you a little visual aid.

You can't go through life on your assets and ignoring your
faults. That's kid stuff! Don't say you want to become an adult
and then run the other way when you find out what it means.
When you begin to grow up, you realize that you have a responsibility to yourself—you have to try to reduce your shortcomings before they overshadw your merits. The best time
to do it is during your young years, before your bad habits
have a chance to dig in. As Dr. Johnson said, "The diminutive
chains of habit are seldom heavy enough to be felt until they
are too strong to be broken."

You're absolutely too young to be a hopeless case, but you
may be in for a struggle. Remember, your bad habits may be
young but they're not feeble—any more than you are! A lot
depends upon your attitude. If you're really determined, you'll
find the stamina you need to break a bad habit. After all, habits
are made through repetition and they have to be broken in the
same way. If you're making only a half-hearted effort, you'll
be ready to give up after your first failure.

A good way to finish off a bad habit is to replace it with a good one. That's an old piece of advice that sounds new every time it's rediscovered! And it works, too!

For most of my life I wasn't exactly a latecomer, but I certainly wasn't a girl you might call punctual, either, and this began to bother me when I looked at my first Miss America itinerary. Unless I could make every minute count, I knew I would have to miss out on some of the exciting things that were crammed into every hour. I just couldn't do that! I didn't want to tangle up the schedules of my chaperones, either.

Well, I had some habit-breaking to do—in a hurry! I made up my mind that this was one Miss America who would arrive on time for every single appointment, no matter what I had to drop to do it. I started the very day after I was crowned, and that wasn't easy. You see, I was crying. I had started to cry the moment I heard my name announced as the winner, and I couldn't stop. I think any girl will understand why I didn't want to go to a press conference—my first one—with red eyes and big wet streams of tears running down my cheeks. Would you want your picture taken if you looked like that?

The conference was about to begin and I knew the reporters had already arrived in the conference room. Finally I reminded myself of my decision to be punctual—that was more important than the way I looked. Besides, I told myself, at the rate I was crying, I might not stop all year!

When I appeared on time that morning, nobody made a fuss about it. And there wasn't any reason for one. The other people at the conference led busy lives, too, yet they managed to get there, and they had every right to expect the same of me. I had won a great honor, an honor that gave me an opportunity to represent the American girl—and she's very dependable!

I stopped crying after a few days, but I didn't stop being on time for appointments. In fact, during my year as Miss America I wasn't late once. Some people say that pressure breaks down the best of habits, but it doesn't have to work that way.

The best time to break in a good new habit is during a time of pressure—if you can stick to it then, the rest is a breeze!

There's no reason why you should put up with your shortcomings when you can train yourself to do so many worthwhile things. Are you the forgetful type? Does your best friend look at you with big sad eyes because you forgot to send her a birthday card? Do you ever envy the girl who seems to remember everything that matters in life? Well, the thoughtful girl wasn't born that way any more than you were born forgetful, but she knows better than to rely on her memory. Even if your memory is like an IBM machine, it's bound to slip up now and then at the most embarrassing times. A notebook and pencil are much better, especially if you're conscientious about jotting down all the things you don't want to forget.

If there is anything more unattractive than thoughtlessness, it's rudeness, and that's downright ugly. The worst part about it is that most people don't realize what they are doing. They're too busy thinking of themselves and their own preferences, and this makes them completely insensitive to other people's feelings. If you know a girl like this, be a real friend and tell her about it.

Even the rudest girl can change her ways if she can be awakened to the fact that other people have feelings like hers. If she will put herself in their shoes for a little while, she might be shocked to discover how often she offends sensitivities by cutting into conversations, plunking herself down in the only comfortable chair, interrupting people while they're concentrating, eating before everyone comes to the table, pushing herself into the cafeteria line, and almost never saying "thank you" for anything. In case this girl doesn't know where to begin to mend her fences, let her take some advice from the most considerate Man who ever lived: "And as ye would that men should do to you, do ye also to them likewise" (Luke 6:31, KJV).

It's good to remember those words whenever you catch yourself making a derogatory remark about someone. Would you like people to tear you down when you're not around?

Neither does anyone else! And you can do them a favor by swallowing the cutting remark before it passes your lips. I agree with the man who said that people were like automobiles —when you hear one knocking all the time, it's a sure sign there's something wrong under the hood!

Be careful not to knock yourself too much. Don't find faults where there aren't any, and try to be graceful about accepting your limitations. Your voice may not be good enough for the lead in the school operetta, but you can do a great job singing in the chorus. If you've always wanted to be a cheerleader, but you're worried about having two left feet, chin up!—I know exactly how you feel! I couldn't move as well as some of the other girls when I was a cheerleader in high school, but I sure could yell loud. I guess that served its purpose, because I made the cheering squad in college, too.

Working with your talents and trouble spots is the best way you can get to know the real you. As you begin to accept your personality for what it is, you will feel it challenging you. You're like a sculptress working with a block of beautiful marble—a little chip here and a little chip there, and the features begin to emerge. Finally, when the chipping is done, the sculptress polishes the marble until all the color and glow deep in the stone shines through to the surface.

I know that some girls don't think they can glow at all, but I disagree with them. I believe that every girl is beautiful— that is, in the true sense of the word. When I talk about beauty, I don't mean the skin-deep kind or the kind that goes on in layers of creams and powders. I'm talking about the beauty that comes from within a girl, the beauty that reflects a completely lovely person. This is the real you—and you're beautiful! God made you that way in the first place.

Without inner beauty, the most stunning face and figure are meaningless. They're also temporary. But inner beauty can stand alone at any age. It expresses a girl's total being and it can even affect the atmosphere in a room full of people. Outer beauty is lifeless and dull—it just sits still and stares out at people. Inner beauty is a bouncy charge of life that reaches out and taps people on the shoulder. It lets the whole world know you're here!

6

What About
the Deep-Down You?

❧ *Beauty is a*

very touchy subject with girls who think they haven't got it.
If they're thinking of beauty in the commercial sense, they
may be right. Not all of us are born with a perfect combination of features.

Unfortunately, the commercial idea of beauty is very shal-
low and it's a shame that so many girls spend so much time trying to achieve it. When you get right down to it, the world's
idea of beauty is nothing more than an appearance, a hard,
brittle, outer shell that can be decorated according to the
latest fad. It has nothing to do with the personality, character,
and integrity of the person who lives deep down inside each
of us.

If you want to pursue the world's idea of beauty, you'll find
plenty of instruction along the way. You can hardly go anywhere without running into an ad that tells you how to become beautiful, more beautiful, or the most beautiful girl in
the world. Beauty is a big business today and it never seems to
have its fill of customers.

Only recently I heard a radio advertisement describing
some back-to-school clothes for little girls. "Mothers," the an-
nouncer said, "send your daughter back to school with a fashionable pencil box designed just like a model's tote bag!" If

you hear enough of these things from the time you're a child, you may grow up to think that beauty comes only on hangers and in tubes.

Take a look at some of our highways and you'll see that the commercialization of beauty can become quite ugly. People are beginning to complain that all those billboards featuring beauty products are covering up the true loveliness of our land.

The same thing can happen to a girl who pursues the phantom of beauty. Most of the time she ends up exhausted and disappointed, and if she somehow achieves the world's ideal of beauty, she has to worry about growing out of it.

There is a kind of beauty that lasts a lifetime. It is the beauty God sees in us, the beauty He gives to each of us. This isn't a feature, like a nose or a mouth, and it doesn't grow automatically over the years. The real beauty in every girl is an elusive inner quality that has to be carefully and prayerfully developed. Only its potential is yours at birth, and you can't ever see it or touch it. It's more of an image—*God's image of you.*

God will always see your real beauty, no matter what you do to cover it up, but who else has His kind of eyes? No one —and surely not you! You could live a lifetime without realizing what a beautiful promise exists inside you. And even though the world is nearsighted, it needs the beauty God sees in you. It needs to see that inner promise fulfilled in your everyday life. If you can begin to live up to God's best hopes for you, the world will know you for what you are—a truly beautiful person.

Yes, you're open to plenty of criticism if you spend hours preparing to face the world, but the beauty inside you needs all the care you can give it. Primping is nothing more than conceit, but the attention you give to your inner self is a form of thankfulness. It shows that you appreciate the qualities God gave you and you want to share them with the rest of the world.

41

Your inner beauty is made up of all the good things about you—your feelings, your hopes, your principles. It is colored by the way you live and it keeps a remarkably good record. If you give way to anger instead of kindness, don't expect to grow in loveliness. If you can put your anger aside and try to be more patient with people, you'll feel beautiful. It sounds quite simple, but it doesn't always work out that way!

It isn't easy to turn your back on the commercial definition of beauty, especially when it seems to fill the whole world with its noise and dazzle. But it might help you to remember another definition of beauty, one that has held up for centuries: "Don't be selfish; don't live to make a good impression on others. Be humble, thinking of others better than yourself. Don't just think about your own affairs, but be interested in others too and in what they are doing" (Philippians 2:3-4, LIVING LETTERS). These are some words from the Apostle Paul in a letter to a Christian congregation during the first century after Christ. I can't think of a better guide to real beauty in any age.

Although very few people talk about the inner beauty as such, they describe it when they talk about personality. How many times you must have heard people say, "She isn't exactly pretty, but what a beautiful personality she has!" They really mean that the girl they admire has allowed her inner beauty to show through. Personality—that much-sought-after phenomenon—is actually the expression of the things God sees in you. If you can reflect this image clearly, you will have a pleasing personality.

Some people have personality problems and they run around in circles trying to solve them. They even take courses designed to improve their personality. If you are one of these people, don't look for help on the outside, because it won't do you any good. Your only reward will be a bad case of tension—and that's a blow to any personality. Look inside yourself to find out what's wrong.

If your inner beauty has been covered over with layers of

resentment, bitterness, selfishness, and a lot of other sour feelings, it isn't surprising that your personality is a complete dud. You may think you can hide these things behind an attractive appearance, but how wrong you are! They show through because they've had the opportunity to curdle your whole being. You may have lived with these feelings so long that you don't notice them—but other people do!

Real beauty never goes unnoticed, even though its commercialized imitation seems to get all the attention. Nobody really wants a counterfeit. You can try to be the show-stopper, the girl whose beauty makes everyone gasp when she enters a room—if that's what you want. But that's such a small goal. Wouldn't you rather be the girl who makes everyone breathe a little easier because they enjoy being in her company?

Inner beauty, like talent, has to be developed with great care, and it calls for more than practice and determination. This isn't a job you can do by yourself, unless you want the kind of beauty that comes in a bottle—and that kind doesn't reflect much of a glow. You'll need help, lots of it, from many different sources, but first of all you'll need people.

7

You and People

❧ *I really enjoy*
people. I welcome every chance I get to talk to them, to learn
about their experiences, their interests—and, yes, even their
problems.

During my year as Miss America I met a great many people
and sometimes felt a little worn out by crowds. Yet, shaking
hands and talking to all the individuals in those crowds never
tired me. Sometimes, when I looked out the plane window as
we were landing and saw a lot of people waiting at the gate,
I wondered if I would have the energy to go out and meet
them. As soon as I got off the plane and walked toward the
gates, everything changed. I could distinguish faces in the
crowd, and an eagerness would come over me. "Hi, Vonda!"
someone would say, and a warm, friendly hand, would grasp
mine. Right then and there, something inside me always re-
sponded by putting a big happy grin on my face, and I felt
refreshed.

People in general can be a little overwhelming if you think
of them as one big blur. If you take them one at a time, and
realize that each time you meet someone you have an opportunity to know a wonderfully new and different creation,
you won't be afraid of crowds. Of course, you're new and
different to other people, too, and you have to give them a
chance to get to know you.

There is no trick to getting along with people but the girl

who won't give it a try is certainly handicapped. Oh, I know all about the values of solitude, and I agree that they're great, but solitude wasn't meant to be a way of life. If we were supposed to be loners, this would be an entirely different world. For one thing, we'd probably still be a little prehistoric. Don't forget, people got together and formed languages, tribes, and cities for more than protection against the elements. They had known what it was to live alone, and they certainly didn't like it!

If you can't be a joiner, you're a bit prehistoric, in a sense. I'm sure you do very well by yourself, and you may get a big kick out of your own company, but have you ever known any other kind? If you gave yourself a chance to mingle with other people, you might find your own company a bit boring after a few minutes.

The girl who says she can do without people is putting up a brave front. We all need each other and we're all good for each other. We need each other's encouragement to try, we need each other's comfort when we lose, and we need to share our victories with each other.

A genuine love for people isn't exactly a spontaneous combustion. You have to *try* to like them, even before you meet them, and this is something everyone can do. It might help if you remember that God loves each and every one of us, and you can surely find something to like in someone He loves.

Maybe you expect too much from people. If you do, then it's your fault that you're always disappointed, isn't it? Do you expect people to offer you instant friendship as soon as you meet them? Do you want them to reassure you, to make you feel important, self-confident? You're asking for a lot—and giving nothing!

You're not the only one who wants to be liked and accepted. Other people want these same things from you, and once you begin to realize this you'll see that you can make a pretty fair exchange. Instead of worrying about whether people will like you, make up your mind that you're going to find

45

something to like in them. Approach them on this basis and you'll feel a difference in your handshake, a new warmth in your smile. You'll see your own friendliness reflected in the faces of other people and, before long, you'll find all the acceptance and fondness anyone could want. Better than that, you'll know that you've made someone else as happy as you are.

I think most of us have especially warm feelings for certain people we have met. Whether we have known them all our lives or only for a few moments, some people seem to bring a smile to our spirits whenever they cross our memories. Have you ever wondered why? I have, and I think I've come up with part of the answer. We simply can't forget the people who were interested in us, the ones who listened to what we had to say, the ones who seemed to think of us as more than faces in the passing crowd.

Jesus had that beautiful quality of being interested in people, and everyone knew it before He said a word. It's right there in the Bible, in all the amazing scenes where people opened up their hearts to a humble Carpenter. They didn't have to know Him for a long time, they didn't have to wonder whether He would be interested in their humdrum lives. They knew He wanted to know all about them, and His love and concern for them changed their lives. They were no longer humdrum. They were people, each one a special and much-loved creation, and they began to take an interest in each other as well as in themselves.

Jesus has that same effect on us today. From the moment you open your heart to Him, you will feel His intense concern for everything you do and you'll begin to give far more serious thought to the way you live. You'll feel important, and you'll be absolutely right—you are very important to Jesus Christ, and so is every other person in this world.

People can make you feel important, but in a quite different way. The more special they make you feel, the more you

46

will find yourself cut off from them. Yes, you can aim for a pedestal, but you'll find it a very lonely place.

There isn't anything lonely about the heart that knows God's love. You can't possibly keep it all to yourself. Instead of cutting you off from people, God's interest in you will make you want to reach out to all the other people He loves, and His love will become the link that connects you with them. You'll begin to see that people don't have to be name-droppers or world travelers to be interesting. They simply have to *be*, that's all.

Again, it's a matter of giving instead of expecting to get—when you give people your attention, you'll find that they really deserve it!

The same thing is true when it comes to helping other people. Some girls have a gloomy view of the world as a kind of battleground where everybody looks out for herself, and nobody else. They'll tell you that when the chips are down, you can't count on anyone but yourself. But I wonder if they've ever reached out a helping hand instead of waiting for one to come their way.

If any girls ever had a reason to turn a deaf ear to a call for help, it was during the Miss America Pageant. *But they didn't!* Most people see only the final hours of the Pageant, but actually it goes on for a whole week before the winner is crowned. For many hours during each day of that week, the contestants are judged, not only for their performances in the talent competitions, but on the other aspects of the Pageant as well—intellect, personality, beauty. Whatever we were doing—whether backstage or out in the middle of the spotlight—we were being evaluated as potential representatives of the ideal American girl. Even if we had butterflies in our stomachs, we were expected to eat our meals in public dining rooms where our table manners were carefully scrutinized. Just try wrestling with a tossed salad without dropping any of it on the formal gown you're required to wear to dinner—

47

and remember to be conversational at the same time—and you'll find it pretty easy to get lost in your own problems.

The competition was keen and each of us was there to contest against the other, or we wouldn't have entered the Pageant in the first place. We had to give so much thought to ourselves and our performances that it seemed impossible to think of anyone else's problems. I suppose most of us expected nothing but a campaign of discouragement from the other girls, so we were in for a surprise.

Instead of finding ourselves in an enemy camp from the moment we arrived in Atlantic City, we found ourselves among friends. No one hoped the others would fall flat on their faces, no one felt superior to anyone else—but all of us were humbled by the quality of the talent we saw!

I will never forget the forty-nine remarkable young women I met in Atlantic City. They became my friends. Each of them was under a lot of strain, but each of them seemed to be more interested in helping the other girls to relax and do their best. Perhaps they even forgot about their own problems in their eagerness to help others.

I was voted Miss Congeniality by the other contestants, but the unselfish friendliness of those girls helped to make me the winner. After all, a vital part of any performer's act is an appreciative audience, and I had the best!

When a girl genuinely likes people, she doesn't usually break under any kind of pressure. In fact, she can take it quite well because she always has a feeling of sharing her experiences, good or bad. It's the loner who has to take the full brunt of pressure, all by herself, and she's the one who's likely to bite your head off when she's under a strain.

If you're a loner, you're missing too much in life. Your own personality will surely suffocate unless it can breathe the fresh air of friendliness, and your inner beauty will wilt in the close quarters of your own little world. If shyness is your excuse, it's a poor one. There's nothing wrong with a shy girl—in fact, she can be very attractive. You can come on strong, if that's your nature, but come on in whatever way is best for you. Give yourself a chance to learn that everyone else has at least a touch of shyness, and they'll welcome your understanding of it.

The best exercise for your personality is people. They are absolutely essential to the development of your inner beauty. I realize this may seem like a big job—and it is—but the hardest part is getting started. Now is the time to start—right where you are, among the most important people in your life.

8

You and Your Home

🌹 *If you put*

your best foot forward only when you step out your front door, you're wasting your time. Unless you can be a beautiful person to your family, you won't impress the rest of the world.

Your family members don't cease to be people simply because they're related to you, but some girls don't seem to realize this. They make the mistake of asking their families to put up with all the faults their friends never get to see. This is wrong, and in the long run it can hurt them. After all, if you can't get along with your family, how will you ever get along with anybody?

Someone always reminds me that I'm on shaky ground when I talk about big families with brothers and sisters—there are only three in my family. Well, I wasn't completely cut off from the rest of the world by being an only child. I had to find some playmates when I was a little girl, and I made friends as I was growing up—and I don't think this is so different from getting along with brothers and sisters!

Your family gives you a wonderful opportunity to learn the meaning of friendship. You're all stuck with each other —and that's just fine! A friend can drop you in a second if she doesn't like the way you blink your eyes, and you may not be able to do anything about it. But your family can't walk out on you, any more than you can walk out on them. When you make mistakes, you'll know it right away and you'll have a chance to make some corrections—because your family is still there. You can also learn something from the mistakes your relatives make—you can learn to forgive.

You may have some complaints about the most important people in your life, but are you so nice to have around the house? If you're busy criticizing your family, where do you find the time to make any improvements on yourself? Do you make your family wonder why you have any friends at all?

Whether you like it or not, your family is a powerful influence on you. Your reactions to them, your deepest feelings about them, shape your personality, and in this way your family becomes an inseparable part of you. Maybe you aren't quite satisfied with your family—well, you can't do anything to change them, but you can change your attitude toward them, and this is very important.

No matter how quarrelsome the family, no matter how torn apart by all kinds of friction, one friendly person can improve the atmosphere. Even if the rest of your family go on with their arguing, at least your voice will be subtracted from the overall roar. In fact, you may find that a soft answer can be the loudest, most persuasive argument you ever heard!

Friendship is something you have to learn by doing. It isn't enough to *have* friends—you must *be* a friend. It isn't enough to have a loving family who dote on everything you do—you have to be someone lovable. Everyone knows that the taker doesn't really get much out of life, but the giver doesn't do much better. It's the girl who learns to give and take who can make friends—in her home and anywhere else. Take your example from the good things your family does, and make yourself a good example for their lives.

If your family gives you a lot of attention, don't be a sponge and soak it all up. They've invested a lot of their love in you because they think you're worthy of it, and you'd better be sure you are. Learn something from the attention you get—learn to pay attention to other people because you know how nice it feels to be in the spotlight.

Open your eyes to the life around you. You'll see that the other people in your home are individuals, too, and they have their rights. Maybe you've been stepping on them and they've been too sweet to complain. The world isn't really a cold, cruel place, but it won't put up with your rudeness, so you'd better watch your manners.

Good manners are like a new pair of shoes. They may pinch a little at first, but you can break them in by wearing them around the house. The world likes polite people, and so does your family, even if they've given up on you. Why not use your manners everyday, wherever you are, until you don't feel comfortable without them.

When you were a little girl, you were probably taught to say "please" when you wanted something. Now, maybe you made a special effort to say it when your family had visitors, but the word was intended for general use and not only for special occasions. Try it on your family now, even for the slightest request, and watch what happens. If their mouths drop open in shock, you've been guilty of gross neglect!

Remember the little courtesies when you're with your family. Introduce your mother and father to your friends, and do it with pride. Ask your sister if you can borrow her plaid skirt—don't raid her closet. Don't humiliate your brother by calling him a pest in front of your friends—and don't do it in private, either, or he may turn into one. If you have grandparents in your home, don't treat them like strangers.

Nobody likes to be nagged, but we often forget that the person who has to do the nagging isn't having a good time, either. If your parents are always on your back, there must be a reason for it. You may be so involved with your own life that you don't realize how inconsiderate you are.

Family life depends on the cooperation of each and every member. When one person disregards the needs of the others, everyone suffers. You may wonder why your mother gets so annoyed when you're only a few minutes late for dinner each night, but you might understand if you looked at life from her point of view. If you've ever cooked dinner for a group of people, you'll understand how she feels. It's no fun to get everything ready at the right time, and put a hot meal on the table, and wonder where everybody is. No one should object if you have a good reason to be late for dinner now and then, but you're being unfair if you make it a habit.

Lots of people joke about girls who monopolize the telephone and the family car, but the jokes haven't solved the problem. You've probably heard all the reasons why you shouldn't be so selfish, and they're all true! But you have your side of the story, too, don't you? Some bits of news won't keep, and you simply have to talk to your girlfriend right away. And why shouldn't you use the car? Everybody else is driving to school!

You're not completely wrong. The telephone and the car belong to the family, and you're a member of it. You have your rights. Yes, you have *your* rights, but not everyone else's rights as well. Things like the telephone are meant to be shared by the whole family, and no one objects to your taking your fair share. The objection comes when you use the telephone so much that no one else can use it.

You've got a real problem. You can't cut yourself off from your friends, but you don't want to be the villain in your family, either. Why don't you be a good sport and take care of your own needs? If you get a small job after school, you can save your money and get your own phone—many girls do. You might try babysitting. Depending upon your thrift, you can even plan to buy your own car someday.

A little independence is good for you, and for your family, too. Yes, families do depend on each other, but they don't have to *lean* on each other. There are some things you have to do for yourself.

I saved for a long time to get my first car, and there will never be another one like it. It was old, scratched, badly in need of paint—and absolutely beautiful to me! After a few months, it began to look beautiful to other people, too. It had

53

a new coat of shocking-pink paint, a new white canvas top, and black and white leather seat covers.

I suppose most girls think of a car in terms of fun, and there isn't anything wrong with this. My perky little car became the favorite of my friends, and even my mother and father enjoyed driving it. But a car is more than a good time—it's a big responsibility, and you'd better learn how to budget your income if you hope to support one. A car needs gas, oil, tires, and repairs, and you're the one who will have to see to its needs.

Maybe you think a car will let you get away from your family more often. Well, think again! When you have a car of your own, you'll be much closer to your parents because you'll begin to assume some of the same responsibilities they've been carrying all these years. You're probably like most other girls, including me, when the family car has to be washed—you disappear! You can't do that with your own car. It'll be sitting right where you left it, just as dirty, when you come back. And when someone else is at the wheel of your very own car, can you remain calm and quiet? I doubt it! You probably say some of the same things your mother says to you when you're driving the family car. When you catch yourself doing these things, you'll realize that your parents are pretty good sports, after all.

It's only natural for families to get involved in each other's lives. This isn't an invasion of your privacy—it's their way of sharing, and you've probably felt the same way about them. When you care about someone, their problems and joys become more important than your own.

Sometimes it's easier to experience something yourself than to watch someone else go through it, so you might try to be more patient when your family seems to hold their breath at every move you make. If advice comes at you from all directions, don't slam your door in your family's face and tell them to mind their own business. You *are* their business! You may not always be able to use the advice they give you, and they may not always understand you, but can you really do without their interest in you? How would you feel if your family didn't care what you do with your life?

Have you ever tried to understand your family? Do you get involved in their lives, or are you lost in your own? When your sister is studying for an exam, do you try to live a little more quietly? And when your mother expects her friends for lunch, do you straighten up your room? In other words, is your life changed by the things that are going on in other people's lives?

You don't really have to understand your family, and they don't have to understand you—you can still love each other. Jesus certainly wasn't understood in His family. Neither His parents nor His brothers realized who He was or what He had come to do, but that didn't lock them out of His life. They worried about Him constantly, sometimes to the point of embarrassment. Imagine how He must have felt when He was preaching in the Temple and saw His mother and brothers standing at the edge of the crowd, beckoning Him to come home! Yes, He spoke sharply to them then, but that was a rare occasion. Most of the time He was patient and gentle.

If you and your family understand each other, you're very fortunate, but you'll still have some problems. You may try to run each other's lives simply because you know what's best for each other.

My family has always been so close that we seemed to know what was going on in each other's minds. We shared everything—laughter, tears, hopes, disappointments—and we tried to do as well in the wings as we did in the spotlight.

We gave each other advice—which we didn't always follow —and we stuck to our opinions when we believed we were right. When we discovered we were wrong, we apologized. Needless to say, I gave more apologies than I received, but my score has been improving over the years.

I'm beginning to realize that it was especially hard for

my parents to stand on the sidelines of my life. How easily they could have solved some of my most difficult problems. But they would have solved them in their way, and they wanted me to find a way of my own. While they always reached out to keep me from falling, they let me stub my toe many a time.

Now I look back and smile because I once thought my parents didn't understand me. How wrong I was! When I bought my little old car, they saw that I was bursting with independence, and while they encouraged me to become self-reliant, they knew that independence and wisdom don't necessarily come together. Naturally, I felt that if I was old enough to buy and drive my own car, I was old enough to go to my performances all by myself. I didn't want my mother or father to come along with me as though I were a baby!

This might have led to a big family disagreement if my parents hadn't been able to see that there was a bit of right on both sides of the issue. I was ready to state my case in the most dramatic terms, and I was slightly deflated when my parents agreed to let me go alone, but I remember thinking that they weren't so old-fashioned, after all. Off I drove in my merry little car, with no one but my dummy on the seat beside me. I felt very mature that night, and even from the stage I was sure that it showed.

I was performing for an adult group at a church and it was dark when I came out to my car, but there were lots of other people in the parking lot. I put Kurley on the front seat and drove away, quite proud of myself. Everything was fine until we turned onto a side street which seemed quite lonely after the busy brightness of the main road. How quiet it was! I tried to start a conversation with Kurley, but he didn't have much to say. I didn't see another car coming in the opposite direction but I felt a little better when the headlights of a car behind me occasionally showed up in the rearview mirror.

Finally I decided that independence wasn't exactly the

breeze I thought it would be. It has its serious side, too. When you are on your own, you begin to notice things you ordinarily wouldn't have seen—such as the darkness. Well, I decided, I had to learn to get along in the darkness as well as in the light. So I began to sing, and pretty soon Kurley joined me in a duet. By the time I drove into our driveway, I was singing at the top of my lungs and having a grand time.

I guess I expected to find my mother waiting at the window, but she had her nose in a book when I walked in. Dad wasn't even home, and when he came in a few minutes later he didn't seem to notice the great change that had taken place in my life. Yes, they were coming along very well.

Little did I realize then that my big adventure was a big concern to my parents. My mother hadn't read a single word of that book, and she had been standing at the window until the moment I drove into view. My father was out, all right—he was out in his car, following me at a discreet distance. The lights in my rearview mirror belonged to his car!

I hadn't fooled my parents with my singing. They remembered how they had felt when they were my age and went out alone at night for the first time. In fact, they had known all along how I would feel, but they also knew I had a right to my own experience.

We all want to grow up, and most of us blame our parents for holding us back. I'm not so sure they really do. Parents usually welcome signs of maturity in their children, even though it may sadden them a little, but their children have mixed feelings about it.

When I was crowned Miss America, I should have been the happiest girl in the world, but I certainly didn't look that way. In fact, I was pretty depressed during the first few days of my reign. My parents had followed my progress through every event of the Pageant, and they went with me to New York where we hoped to spend some days together before I began my tour of the country. College and the Pageant had taken me away from home during most of the previous year, and I was beginning to miss it. I dreaded the day when my parents were to fly back to Phoenix.

After our first day in New York I knew our family reunion would have to wait. I was separated from my parents by a barrier of reporters, photographers, waiters, fitters, advertising representatives, Pageant officials, chaperones, and well-wishers, and we were lucky to pass each other in the hall now and then. I had so many appointments, one right after the other, that I couldn't get out of my hotel for a moment, and I thought wistfully of my parents as they went out to explore the city.

"Look like a queen!" the photographers kept saying, but I began to feel more and more like a little girl, even though I realized how foolish I was. Ever since my childhood I had wanted to become Miss America, but now that I had, I didn't seem to fit the title. Miss America had to be a much more mature girl than I was!

It wasn't until later that I learned how difficult those days had been for my mother and father, especially when they were trying to look happy for my sake. Even from a distance they sensed what was going on in my mind and heart, and if they had looked upon me as a little girl I think they would have said, "Oh, come on home with us!"—and at that moment, I might have gone!

On the night before they were to leave for home, my parents worked their way into my schedule and took me out to dinner in a famous restaurant. That did it! As soon as we walked in, a waiter recognized me and greeted me by my title, and somehow that made it real. I was exactly what I had wanted to be, and my parents had helped me to achieve my goal. I had a responsibility to them as well as to the little girl who dreamed a dream.

For several days, I had only picked at my food, but that night I made up for all the meals I had missed. I ate everything in sight! Then I looked at my mother and father and

58

saw a mixture of pride and sadness in their eyes, and I knew that I had no reason to be homesick. Home is something you carry around with you—in your heart!

When I said good-bye to my parents at the end of the week, I felt that I was going to burst with my love for them. And then I recalled an amusing and astute article I had cut out of a newspaper and pinned on my bulletin board a few years ago:

MY PARENTS

At 7—My parents are the smartest people in the world. They know everything.

At 17—My parents don't know as much as I thought they did.

At 21—My parents don't know anything, compared to me. They just don't understand the younger generation.

At 35—My parents knew much more than I thought they did. They were really quite worldly-wise.

At 50—My parents were always right. Everything they did was for my benefit.

I knew I had made a discovery the newspaper article didn't mention—my parents were my friends!

9

You and Your Friends

❧ *When you make*

friends outside your family, you have to start from scratch.
They don't live with you; they don't even have to put up with
you at all unless you offer them something worthwhile as a
person.

If you're on friendly terms with your family, you shouldn't
have any trouble getting along with other people. The question is, how many other people?

Some girls will tell you that you shouldn't scatter your attention among too many people because you'll never have
enough time to build any lasting friendships. Better to have
a few close friends, these people say, and let the rest of the
world go by.

On the other side of the fence are those who say you should
meet as many people as you possibly can, and try to make
friends with all of them. Beware of the possessive friendship,
they'll tell you, and don't let it narrow your life.

Well, there's a lot of sense in both arguments, and the final
decision is up to you. But I really don't see why you can't
follow both bits of advice and lead a very happy life. True, it
takes time and thought and care to build a single friendship,
but it doesn't take a whole lifetime! With so many years ahead
of you, you'll have time to build several friendships of the best
kind.

What about all those other people you'll meet? Should

you turn your back on them because you don't have time to get to know them well? Can't you squeeze them into your life, too? Yes, you certainly can! You can make acquaintances as well as friends, and you don't have to pass up anybody.

Acquaintances are people you'd like to know better if you had the opportunity—but you don't. You may see them for a few minutes every day of your life, or only long enough to say "hello," but you have the feeling that if you could share your thoughts with them, you would find some new friends.

Friends need more of your time. You can't wave to them every day and let it go at that. You have to give something of yourself to your friends, and part of them must become part of you. This is where you have to be careful. Your friends can add to the loveliness growing inside you by liking you for your best qualities, or they can shrivel up your beauty by encouraging you to be your worst.

Not that friends won't tolerate your faults—they will, if your assets outweigh them. That's part of being a friend, and you should remember that it works the other way around. A friend, as someone once said, is the girl who doesn't think you've done a permanent job when you've made a fool of yourself. Remember to be this kind of person when your friends make their share of goofs.

The more friendships you make, the more easily you'll be able to make them. As in everything else, experience is a marvelous teacher, probably because it overcomes the shyness that makes us hold ourselves back from people. You're not alone if you feel clumsy when meeting people—you have lots of company, including me. Maybe everyone else seems to make friends as naturally as they breathe air, but they weren't always that way.

I was never exactly shy with people, but I used to feel a little awkward about meeting them. I never knew what to say. Other people always seemed to say the right words and in the right order, and this made me very impatient with myself. Then one day I took a good look around and saw that I wasn't the only girl in the world who had a problem. A few others were having the same kind of troubles and we had one thing in common—our lack of experience.

When we're very young, we don't have to worry about meeting people because our parents are usually with us and they help us over the rough spots. In fact, we can sit still and let our parents do all the talking for us. But when we grow up and begin to make friends on our own, it's only natural for us to feel a bit self-conscious. After all, we're putting ourselves up for approval, aren't we?

It's hard to think of anything but yourself when you first begin to approach people on your own. You're worried about the impression you're going to make, and you're probably trying too hard to make it a good one. Then you find that you've suddenly picked up some alarming physical handicaps —moist palms, dry throat, rubbery knees, and a shrill laugh you've never heard before. Who on earth could possibly approve of *you!* Well, you may be surprised. You're going through something everyone can understand.

The girl who takes your moist hand and grasps it firmly as she looks into your eyes with genuine interest can certainly sympathize with you because she's gone through the same experience many times—so many, in fact, that it no longer bothers her. That's the only difference between your awkwardness and her ease. You probably find that hard to believe right now, but one of these days—if you keep on meeting people—you'll be able to see the transformation in yourself.

You don't have to sit and wait for it to happen. You can help yourself along by accepting the fact that you're going to be a bit jittery about meeting people, and in that way you can take some of the pressure off yourself. Try to think of the person you're meeting instead of worrying about yourself. Don't tie yourself up into a pretzel by wondering what you're going to say. You don't even know what the other person is going to say, and that might have a lot to do with your reply.

62

Of course, if you always wait for someone else to speak the first word, you may wait forever. What about the girl who sits next to you in chemistry? She might turn out to be a lifelong friend if only you could find a reason to talk to her. Why do you need a reason? All you need is one word—"hello"—and perhaps a smile. One of you has to say it first, and it might as well be you.

Try to relax and let your real personality make friends for you. One of these days you'll be the girl with the firm handshake and the steady voice. You'll realize that meeting people can be fun, and you'll make an extra effort to be friendly to that pleasant little girl with the shaky knees.

Friendship is so much more than a word, a handshake, and a smile. It's the ability to see the inner beauty in someone. Yes, people have faults, but you don't have to be blinded by them. When you see something good in a girl, compliment her—then you're encouraging her to live up to it. You'd feel the same way if someone believed in you.

What about disagreements? Do they belong among friends? They certainly do, if the friends are still individuals. Your friends are going to look at things in different ways, and you'll have to respect their right to do it. Sometimes you may change your mind and see things their way, but don't feel like a traitor if you don't. A little difference of opinion doesn't mean the end of a friendship—unless the friendship never really existed.

Don't ask your friends to take criticism if you can't. I know you're only trying to be helpful when you tell your friend that yellow isn't her color, but unless you expect her to be equally candid, keep your opinions to yourself! Actually, criticism belongs in a friendship, just as much as praise does, but only when it is given lovingly.

A friend is someone who roots for someone else, and this is so much better than rooting for yourself. The most special achievement in the world can lose its excitement if you're the only one around to enjoy it. But try sharing your victories with a friend, and you'll really begin to understand what they mean! In fact, you'll get a double portion of happiness when your friend shares her joys with you, too.

Friends have to understand each other if they are going to share their experiences. You can't very well give your friend the encouragement she needs if you don't know what she hopes to achieve, and she can't give you the congratulations you deserve if she doesn't know what you have won. Friends have to know what's important to each other.

Do you behave like a clam with your friends? Do your goals seem insignificant compared to theirs? Do you start to give your opinion and then change your mind because your words begin to sound foolish to you? Then you're not anybody's friend!

Friends should be comfortable with each other. Even if their goals are different, they have to respect each other's devotion to them, and feel free to talk about the important things in their lives. If you can't talk about the things that matter to you when you're with your friends, then how can you be yourself in their company? And if you can't be yourself with your friends, how will you ever manage to develop a lasting friendship.

You can get into a habit of pushing your real personality out of sight if you try to make friends with people who only try to please each other. Then, one day, you'll look at yourself in the mirror and wonder where your identity went. You'll try to build a new personality, but it won't be anything like the wonderful one God gave you. You'll tell yourself that you're doing all right. You've got lots of friends, haven't you? And how long do those friendships last? Jealousy, selfishness, impatience, and anger break them up pretty quickly, don't they?

You won't have any of these problems if you make your friendships among people who try to please God. He is pleased by the best things in people—by their honesty, generosity, loyalty, love—and these are the qualities that make good friendships, too.

I often wondered, during my first months as Miss America, what my friends were thinking of me. They must have read some of the press releases that were sent back to my hometown, and I wondered whether they were pleased or disappointed with the way I was wearing my crown. I had hoped that my title would give me a better opportunity to do the things God wanted me to do, but the days came and went in such a whirl that I couldn't be sure I was succeeding.

It was six weeks after the Pageant before I went home for a short visit. This was to be my big test. If my friends felt awkward with me, then I had exchanged my personality for a crown and lost more than I could ever regain.

I wasn't prepared for the scene at the Sky Harbor Airport when my plane landed. Bad weather had made us two hours late, so I didn't expect many people except my family to be waiting for me. I was very sleepy when I got off the plane, but the sudden music of a band jolted me awake. People were coming up the staircase to greet me and behind them were more people, so many of them—smiling, waving, calling! This was my homecoming day, and my town had made it official.

I certainly lived up to my reputation—again I began to cry, and the tears slipped down my cheeks for the entire length of a parade through Phoenix. This time I had company. My parents were crying, my friends were crying, and even some people I had never seen had tears in their eyes. My mother and father had brought my dog Vivi along to the airport because they knew how much I had missed her, and she jumped into my arms as soon as she saw me. She had recognized me, and that was a good sign!

Going home as a celebrity makes a difference. You're almost a guest in your own home and it's hard to talk about the things that are on your mind. My mother and father hardly had a chance to say more than a word, and my friends always seemed to be off in the distance. But they didn't intend to stay there.

So many people wanted to say "hello" and wish me a good year, and I welcomed the chance to thank them for the support they had given me during the Pageant. Finally I turned and saw the familiar smile of my best friend. For a moment we stood there, looking at each other, with a big question mark between us—"Are you the same girl I used to know?"

I don't remember who moved first, but both of us threw our arms around each other and began to talk as though we had never been separated! We had stored up so much news—news that only friends can exchange with each other.

Well, I knew then that I was changing—and in the right direction. I also knew that I would have to work still harder to put my principles into practice during the months ahead. And if I didn't continue to live up to the things they expected of me, my friends would tell me. I could count on them—they looked out for me.

10

You and Your Date

❧ *Wherever Miss*

America goes, young people ask her questions about dating. It's one of the most talked-about subjects today, and most of the girls I met were very tense about it. Their questions always began with "Should I—?" or "Shouldn't I—?"

Before I say anything else, let me say that the decision is up to you. Yes, I know, that's an answer nobody likes to hear, as I discovered. But it's true. No matter how many opinions you may seek out, no matter who may influence you, the choice is yours alone.

Did you ever stop to realize that you may not have much of a choice to make? Everybody knows what they *should* do—unless they've been brought up in a cave out of reach of any human beings. Think about it for a moment. If you've come this far in your life, you know what's right and wrong because the world has been giving you lessons ever since your first day on earth.

The decision has to be made when it comes to *doing* what you know you should do. That's where the trouble begins. That's where dating runs into the kind of problems no girl can solve.

For instance, you know that you *should* ask your young man to call for you at your home when you have a date. You may have all kinds of reasons for not wanting to go along with this admittedly old-fashioned routine, but they probably aren't good ones. Is there something wrong with the boy? Is he rude? Does he make fun of your family? If so, then don't have him call for you. Don't even go out with him!

If you're proud of the boy you're dating, then you should be eager to have your family meet him. They'll have even more respect for you when they see that you have such good taste. You'll also get a chance to look at the young man more objectively when you watch how he behaves with your mother and father. Be sure he's courteous to those sisters and brothers, too.

Some girls are very annoyed when their parents insist on meeting the boy they're dating, and this is a big mistake. It's wonderful to have parents who are interested in your life, and their concern about your acquaintances is a sign of their deep love for you. How would you feel if they couldn't take the time to meet your date? And how would your date feel? Wouldn't he get a bad impression of you?

It's not hard to figure out what you should do about having a boy call for you, but going steady is a more complicated problem. Everybody's talking about it—parents and civic leaders, as well as young people—and there are good reasons pro and con.

Going steady can certainly tie you down and box you in, especially if you begin at an early age. You see the same boy all the time and you never get a chance to compare him with anyone else. You also run the risk of getting too serious much too soon.

I think parents are right to worry about young people who give each other rings or pins or some other pledge of their devotion. It takes all the lightheartedness out of their dating and it makes them very self-conscious. They begin to feel that they have taken a serious step in life and they wonder whether they should take the next one.

If wearing a pin or a ring constitutes "going steady," then I've never done it! Yes, I had a boyfriend in high school. We dated each other regularly, but neither of us liked the phrase

68

"going steady"—it was too uncomfortable. We had seen what happened to some steadies when the going got rough— the jealousies, the break-ups, the agony, the anger—and our lives simply had no room for such things. We were having too much fun! We were favorites with each other, that's all. We didn't think of pins or rings or any other gadgets because they would have cheapened our friendship. After all, if our affection and admiration for each other couldn't keep us together, what good would a ring do?

I know that some people think a girl should get around and meet a lot of different boys before she settles down to one, but playing the field can be dangerous, too. For one thing, you don't get the opportunity to know any boy well enough to relax when you're with him—everything is too stilted and formal. Then you find you're getting a reputation for being flighty, and that attracts the wrong kind of boys.

The worst part of ruling out a boyfriend in your social life is the way you stare at the telephone, especially during the weeks before your friend's big party. It has a way of ringing for everyone else but you, and this can destroy a girl's confidence. If you have a boyfriend, or a favorite date, you're on pretty casual terms with each other and you don't have to wait for a formal invitation to a big event. You simply confirm the fact that you'll both be attending it, that's all.

Having a boyfriend didn't necessarily keep me from the company of other young men while I was in high school and college. Since my boyfriend and I didn't put a label on our preference for each other's company, we didn't feel possessive. In fact, we had a better time when we were with a lot of other young people.

A date doesn't have to be something secluded—it should be something that you and your young man enjoy doing together. It doesn't have to be a special kind of activity or the sort of thing you couldn't enjoy doing with a girlfriend. So many young people think they have to pair off or go off by themselves when they're on a date, and this can lead to trouble.

A curfew is another old idea that is more of a help than a hindrance. Don't pout and argue when your parents tell you to be home at a certain time—agree to it and see that you carry out your promise. Some parents feel uncomfortable about setting a curfew and so they leave it up to the girl, which doesn't help her at all.

I used to complain about my parents' "early-hour" rule, but one day I was able to thank them for it. Let's face it— some dates turn out to be very disappointing, and an early curfew hour can spare you a little boredom. It also lets you end the date without hurting a boy's feelings. If your date turns out to be even better than you thought he would, again you can be thankful for a curfew—the young man will want to see you again, and mighty soon!

Maybe you haven't had enough experience to appreciate the practical virtues of a curfew, but even if you think your parents are being stuffy, don't discuss your objections in front of your date. And don't complain on the way home. Your parents have placed their confidence in you, and you owe them your loyalty. If they haven't told you when to come home, why not impose your own curfew on a date? Just tell the young man—and your parents—what time you plan to come home.

Your reputation is in your own hands, and when you are out on a date you are completely responsible for it. Don't put the burden on the boy—he'll usually follow your lead. After all, he has no other choice, if he wants to see you again.

But suppose you want to see him again? That's the real problem, isn't it? We girls have to wait to be asked, and that isn't easy to do. Sometimes it makes a girl panic and begin to doubt her own principles. If she thinks her standards may slow down her social life, she may throw them aside and do the things that are supposed to make her popular.

How wrong can a girl be! Popularity means so many different things, depending upon the circumstances. Take the matter of petting, for example. Yes, I suppose a certain num-

70

ber of girls become popular because they don't draw the line at petting—but is this the kind of popularity you want?

Again, it's a matter of making up your mind. You know how you *should* behave when you're out with a boy, and you know that you *shouldn't* ever do anything that will cost you his respect. So there really isn't any confusion about the harm you can do to yourself if you let a date end as a petting session. Yes, you may become popular if you give up your principles, but popular with whom? Do you think the special someone of your dreams is going to like a girl who throws her affections around like a bag of confetti? I doubt it!

Take another look at the girls who seem to be so popular because they have a reputation for giving a boy a good time. Yes, they may have as many as twenty dates in a row, while you may have only one now and then—but what happens after a few more weeks? Suddenly a lot of new girls are the popular ones and the others may have to wait months or even years for another date. Don't forget that the type of young man who tries to talk a girl into petting is the kind who gets bored very easily. He gives nothing and takes all, and that can be pretty monotonous for him. Unless he wants to admit that he's at fault, he has to blame his boredom on the girl and convince himself that it's time for a change.

There's so much talk today about the "new" morality, but I think that's just a fancy label for an attempt to get around the old morality. Some things in life don't change, and one of them is the harm that can come to a girl who tries to get around the "should's" in her life. Morality, old or new, is your protection against some ugly forces in life—forces that could destroy the young beauty growing up inside you. Don't let a few words talk you out of your personality, your uniqueness, and all the hopes God has for you.

Affection is a warm, wonderful feeling—until it is used in the wrong way. Petting is so easy to start, and you'll meet with plenty of opportunities to begin, but it can become a dangerous habit that is very difficult to break. Even if you succeed in getting rid of the habit, you're stuck with the reputation that came with it.

Pick your dates carefully, even more carefully than you pick your friends. And remember that a date should be an extension of a friendship if it is to be the kind of experience you can enjoy. Some girls are very casual about the boys they date, perhaps because they don't want to think about boys in serious terms until they're older. Well, in one respect they're right—they don't have to be serious while they're young. But they do have to be responsible. Naturally, you shouldn't think in terms of marriage when you accept a date to go bowling with the gang, but someday you're going to marry one of the boys you date—that's how it happens. You really can't afford to go out with just anybody, can you? You really can't take any chances at all!

You have to think of your future when you accept a date. The young man doesn't have to be that special someone, but he has to be in the same category. If you make a habit of dating boys of different backgrounds, principles, and convictions, then one of these days you're going to face a trying decision.

In our family we have devotions and family prayer after breakfast, and over the years I have found these moments to be a source of great peace and strength. At our family altar we pray for each other and with each other. These are the sort of things I would want to bring to the home I will establish someday with my special someone, and I really can't envision a marriage without them. I would want to teach my children the things of God as I learned them in my home. I would want them to experience the companionship with Christ that I know.

Now, I would have to give up all these plans if I were to marry someone who does not know God as I do—and I don't see how I could possibly do that. Actually, I couldn't, but I would have to come to that decision through a lot of pain that I would rather avoid. I would also have to hurt another person, and there again I would be hurt, too. These are some problems I'll never have to face if I do a little thinking before accepting a date.

If you're old enough to date, you're old enough to have a pretty good set of principles. This is your chance to try them out. Lots of people will tell you how to behave with a young man but you'll have to speak for yourself when you're out with him.

Don't be fooled by the kind of popularity that comes in the door when principles go out the window. It's not your type. You want something that lasts, something that can lead to friendship. You want the kind of popularity that comes to a girl who takes her principles along with her on every date.

11

You and School

🌹 *I was away*

from college for a year while I was Miss America, and I suppose some girls would say I was fortunate—but I missed it. In fact, I didn't even take a vacation when my reign was over. I went straight back to the classroom.

In a way, I really have been fortunate—I've always enjoyed going to school. I realize that some people find it a grind, but I could never understand why. School is full of opportunities to develop yourself and there are so many courses suited to your special preferences. It's quite amazing to realize that there can be so much concern for individuality in such a vast educational system!

Your brain isn't the only thing that can get a workout in school. You also have the chance to make important social adjustments, to learn how to get along with other people, to become a member of a team. It's a wonderful place to put your personality to work.

There is a lot of emphasis on scholarship these days, which isn't strange. The world is becoming more complicated every day and we have to be able to understand the fascinating new subjects that become parts of our lives. But learning isn't restricted to books—it has a lot to do with people.

Go ahead and be a bookworm, if that's what you like. My hat's off to you! But don't stop there. Good grades are vital to your future, and you ought to make every effort to get them

—just don't forget to get in on those extracurricular activities, too. Your studies will help your mind to mature, but your personality grows through experiences with people.

It would be hard to find a talent that couldn't benefit from an education. I've been an active ventriloquist during most of the years I've been in school, but I doubt that I would have been a successful one if I hadn't studied some subjects that helped me to polish my technique. For instance, I studied voice, music, and drama in heavy doses and they certainly taught me how to put variety into my act. They also made me realize that I didn't have to stick to ventriloquism all my life.

Even though I liked school, I must admit that some courses didn't make my life easier. We all have different aptitudes and I found that I simply couldn't grasp some subjects that were a snap for my friends. Did this ever happen to you? If not, you're unusual.

You can't very well sit and sulk when you don't like one of your courses. Yet you can't get a diploma by choosing only the subjects you like. You have to take the good with the bad —and that's a good experience for you.

A difficult course may put a strain on you, but you don't have to suffer. There's a way out. If you look for something enjoyable in that course—even the slightest thing—you'll begin to find the whole course more interesting, and that's the important breakthrough! When you like something, it arouses your interest, and interest is the key to learning.

The hardest part of school is staying in it when you begin to think you've learned all you need to know. There are so many dropouts these days! Everyone is in such a hurry to get going in life that they have no patience with preparation.

I seemed to have everything when I became Miss America, and some people wondered whether I would really go back to college the next year. I suppose I wondered about it, too, although not consciously. I was already doing most of the things I had wanted to do, and there seemed to be no further need for preparation. Then one day I made some television commercials and I got a chance to see highly trained people at work in the field I was hoping to enter.

It's fascinating to watch people who know what they're doing—their actions have a rhythm, an ease about them—and I received an advanced education in television techniques right on the spot. I knew what to do as Miss America but someday I would be Vonda Kay Van Dyke again, and she had a lot to learn about television! My school days most certainly weren't over!

Impatience is only one of the reasons why young people drop out of school and it probably doesn't claim as many victims as the desire for money. Some young people leave school because they have to take jobs to help support their families, and this is the kind of emergency everyone can understand. But these dropouts are usually the ones who finish their education in night school. There is another kind of money problem that causes dropouts—the living-beyond-your-allowance kind of problem—and these dropouts hardly ever come back to get their diplomas.

You're not abnormal if you have ambition. Of course you want to try out your skills in a job and earn your own way in the world. Most of us don't like to make demands on our parents, no matter how generous they are, and after a while we find that our allowances don't cover our growing needs. Some of us would even prefer to pay for our own clothes because it would make us feel more mature.

The willingness to take on adult responsibilities is a very good sign in any girl, and if it's popping up in your life, don't try to hide it. You can pay for part of your own way and still stay in school, which is where you belong. Don't forget that a small paycheck might look big to you now, but unless you finish school you won't ever get a bigger one!

Money is something you should learn to manage at an early age, or it will manage you. It has a place in life but not at the top of the list. It can be very useful in many ways, particularly when you want to help people.

You're old enough to learn what to do with the money you have. And you're old enough to earn the money you need—provided your needs are realistic. As nice as your family may be, don't keep running to them for another raise. Try earning one for yourself.

12

You and Your Job

❧ *Does the thought*
of a job appeal to you? Would you like to earn some money of your own and enjoy the feeling of independence? Then what are you waiting for?

Some girls have the wrong ideas about working after school. They seem to think there's something degrading about it. Well, I suppose it does indicate that you need money—but who doesn't? Whether you need money to buy food, to pay the rent, to buy a car or a new coat, to pay for a college education, or to set yourself up in business—the need is perfectly legitimate.

Suppose your parents are ready to send you to college—wouldn't you like to pay part of your own way? Your parents can always find another use for the money they saved, and they might even find someone who needs it more than you do. No matter how secure your family's finances are, the cost of a college education is a strain. The money has to come from somewhere, and sacrifices always have to be made, even if you aren't aware of them.

From the day I was born, my parents planned to send me to college, and they worked and saved to make that plan a reality. But they also gave me plenty of opportunities to learn to take care of myself, and I thought that their money should go to a need that was more urgent than mine. I wanted to pay my own way—all of it!

If you've been toying with the idea of working a few hours a week after school, get serious about it! You won't find it drudgery, not if the job is interesting, and if you look hard enough you'll find one that is just right for you. It may even give you a chance to work in the field you're studying—such as nursing, recreational counseling, merchandising, teaching.

You may think your time is tied up with studies and extra-curricular activities, but can't you find a few hours that are going to waste? Wouldn't you like to do something useful with them?

There's a certain satisfaction that comes with a paying job. You'll find that the standards are quite high. People will be patient with you because you're a beginner, but don't take advantage of their sympathy. A real job isn't kid stuff!

Your first pay can be a big thrill. It seems like such an enormous amount of money—until you discover how far it has to stretch. Don't forget that working increases your expenses—you now have to pay for transportation, and your clothing will wear out faster.

Girls have an advantage over boys in getting spare-time jobs. Girls can baby-sit, and I don't know what we'd ever do without it! Of course, there's no reason why boys can't baby-sit, too, but very few of them ever do. Maybe they don't want the responsibility. It's a big one. The baby-sitter is a substitute parent, and that calls for special qualifications.

Your college education is probably the biggest expense you can ever tackle, so you'd better think carefully before you pledge yourself to it. If your parents are standing by to help when you're running low on funds, that's wonderful—and you shouldn't hesitate to call on them. But some families have other responsibilities that have first claim on their financial resources, and you may have to stand or fall on your own.

Going away to college is an exciting experience, but not everyone can afford such an expensive education. You stand a better chance of paying your own expenses if you choose a college near your home, especially if it is a community- or state-supported institution.

The Miss America Pageant offers large amounts of scholarship money, and this is one of the major attractions to the girls who compete in it. A girl can feel proud of her achievements if she qualifies as a contestant, because the Pageant has very high standards, and she will then have opportunities to win scholarships from the local contests on up to the National Finals. During the past twenty years, the Miss America Pageant alone has awarded 5.6 million dollars in scholarship money —which makes it the largest women's scholarship foundation in the world. That's quite a record!

Scholarships gave me a lot of help in college. When I won the Arizona Junior Miss title during my senior year of high school, a $250 scholarship came with it. Then came the larger award—one-thousand dollars—with the title of Miss Arizona during my junior year of college.

I'm only one of many girls who have been able to further their education and know the satisfaction of earning the money to pay for it. Some of us have gone on to get advanced degrees and many of us are passing our knowledge on to other young people through teaching careers. This is why I get a little impatient with people who don't take the time to understand the real meaning of a beauty pageant. If they could get to know some of the young women I've met, they would realize that it takes more than a parade to win the interest of such talented, intelligent, and dedicated girls. I never met one contestant who had an insignificant goal.

Money is nice to earn and nice to have, but you shouldn't let it fly out of your hands without a good reason. It has a way of giving you a passing glance if you don't learn how to use it properly.

Once upon a time my parents gave me an allowance of twenty-five cents a week. Now, that was a very big sum of money to a little girl, and I struggled through many a decision about the way it was going to be spent. Only part of it never gave me any trouble—the ten percent that I gave back to God.

I still give God a tenth of my income and I always will. But I don't deserve any credit for doing it, because I'm only returning the money to its rightful Owner. The other ninety percent belongs to God, too, but He has entrusted it to me. It is my job to make good use of that money, to use it for Him to accomplish the things He wants done in this world. Naturally He expects me to use a certain amount for my living expenses, but I'm not supposed to pad the account.

Extravagances aren't out—not entirely, that is. A girl can afford a few little extravagances if she has some money left over after giving ten percent to her church, paying for her education and any other obligations, and providing herself with life's necessities. Sometimes it's good to give yourself a small gift, especially if it has some special significance. I felt just a bit guilty about it, but when I was in Japan as Miss America I put my own name at the bottom of my gift list. When I had taken care of my family and friends I bought myself a tiny transistor TV set which was to go in my dormitory room when I returned to college. I felt terribly extravagant at the time, but my gift to myself turned out to be very practical, after all.

Maybe you think that ten percent is a lot of money to give up. Well, it is, and it's not supposed to go unnoticed in your life. Whenever you follow God's will for your life, you'll be very much aware of it, especially if you have to make some sacrifices along the way. Following God's will isn't like sleepwalking—you're wide awake and looking all around. You're conscious of everything you do and you keep looking for signs that you are going in the right direction.

You won't miss that ten percent, unless you're a very selfish person—and if you *are* selfish, you won't enjoy using your money at all. Don't forget that you wouldn't have any money at all if God hadn't given you the ability to live in this world.

It's His world, you know. You're a visitor here and you came well equipped. You have a body, a mind, and a spirit, plus many gifts of talent, aptitude, skill—all of them given to you by a loving God. Is it asking too much to return to Him a small portion of all you earn with your many blessings?

13

You and God

❧ *God wants much*

more than ten percent of your income. He wants more than your talent, your prayers, your time, your service, or even your love. God wants your life—all of it!

When I was a very little girl I called myself a Christian. I went to church and Sunday school, I prayed and listened to the prayers of my family, and I loved to hear my parents read the Bible aloud. Sunday was the most important day in the week because that was the day when we met with a lot of other people to worship God. Being a Christian was a way of life, I thought, but that shows how little I knew about it.

Being a Christian is life itself, and this is what I began to discover when I was nine years old. My parents took me to a city-wide religious crusade where they were to sing in the choir, and it was then I learned that a Christian faith was something that happened deep inside a person. I remember sitting very still as the preacher spoke of the great change that comes over the person who lets Christ come into his life, and gradually I became aware of a new and beautiful feeling coming over me. I was too young to put it into words, but it gave me a happiness greater than any I had ever known.

It may seem unusual for a child to speak of peace, since that is apparently the last thing in the world children want to experience, but that was the way I described my joy at that moment. At the close of the service, when the call went forth to people to come forward and dedicate their lives to God, I got up and moved toward the aisle, squeezing sideways to avoid the knees and feet of the other people in the row. From the choir my parents watched me, but they didn't try to stop me. They understood. This was my hour of decision!

Afterwards, my pastor explained some of the things I had felt when I made my decision. Children have a way of seeing things very clearly, and while the preacher was speaking of the joy of being a true Christian, I was beginning to realize what I had been missing. I could recite many Bible verses, and I knew lots of hymns, and I was never at a loss for words when I prayed. But my life had not been influenced by any of these experiences—I hadn't *lived* them. I simply wasn't giving enough to God.

When you give your whole life to God, He begins to tell you what to do. You're not the boss any more, and that's a great relief! You'll be shocked when you look back and realize how clumsily you were trying to run your life.

The peace I felt when I stood up to commit my life to God was different from anything I had ever known. It wasn't the kind of peace we can get from other human beings, and it had nothing to do with the absence of noise. I had always known a lot of love in my home, but this was a love that surpassed anything on earth. It made me want to shout with the pure joy of being alive! All of a sudden there was a purpose in the life of a little nine-year-old girl.

So many young people are looking for a purpose in their lives. It's one of the things that make them so restless, so troubled, and so angry. No one likes to feel useless, yet that's the only future so many young people see ahead of them. Everyone tells them to prepare themselves, to study, to develop their characters and their abilities—but for what? The biggest question among young people today is "What am I doing here?" and they aren't getting any answers.

There's only one answer and you can't get it from your

family, your friends, or any other person on earth. The answer can come only from God.

You *are* pretty useless all by yourself. But when you put your future in God's hands you become a different person. You don't struggle with decisions any more and you stop wondering what's going to happen to you. Nothing can frighten you, nothing can get you down, because you know that Someone is watching over you, taking care of you, guiding you every step of your way through life.

Maybe you don't like the thought of letting someone else help you make your decisions. Well, I wouldn't like it either, if it had to be another human being. We're all imperfect, but at least I'm on familiar terms with my own faults—I wouldn't want my life to depend on someone else's poor judgment. But God isn't just another person. He is love itself and He is absolutely perfect. His judgment is flawless and He'll never let you down.

Even though you may have the best intentions, you can make all the wrong moves in your life. Even though you try to live up to your best qualities, you'll find yourself giving in to your worst ones. This is why decisions can be such agonizing moments in a young person's life. You keep wondering whether you've made the right choice, not only for your life but for the lives of all you love.

You can relax when you let God decide for you. Don't let Him help only with big decisions—let Him handle all the little ones, too. He's interested in every moment of your life and He deserves to share in each of them.

No one can give you as much sympathy as God can. He knows exactly how you feel, even though He is perfect and you are so full of faults. He created you, yes, but He did far more than that. He sent His only Son to pay the debt you would have inherited from the sin Adam committed. Jesus died on the cross in your place—and in the place of every other child of God. Your debt is paid, wiped out. Have you ever known a greater love?

God did still more for you. Jesus died, but not forever. God raised His Son from the dead and Jesus lived again. He lives today, and He will come into your life when you give that life to God. Then you too can look forward to eternal life.

I've always noticed that some young people think Jesus prefers the company of adults. If that's what you think, you're so wrong! He's the Best Friend a teen-ager—or any other "ager"—can have.

If you ask Christ to come into your life, you will meet a Friend who "sticketh closer than a brother"—or any other member of your family, no matter how much they love you. There is no love like God's and this is what Christ brings into your heart. It's a love that spills over into all the other lives that touch yours.

A good friend can listen patiently to your problems, and she can even offer some helpful advice, but let's face it—we can't always put our real troubles into words. Sometimes we don't even know what they are, and in our confusion we may carry on about a lot of things that aren't important.

You can talk to Jesus without saying a word. He knows the cause of your trouble long before you do and He knows what to do about it. You may not agree with His solution and you may have some ideas of your own, but you'll change your mind in a little while. Once you let Jesus guide you, you'll see that He's always right.

If you want to look up to someone, look up to Christ. Make Him the model for your life and you will be truly beautiful. You're in for a big struggle if you try to make it on your own, and frankly, you don't have much of a chance to succeed. With Christ as your Guide, you can discover the real joy of living. It isn't a somber, tragic existence—it's full of laughter, and action, and expectation.

Of course your years are empty if the only light you have is from the additional candles on your birthday cake. You can become the biggest success in history and you'll still be very small and insignificant—except in the eyes of God.

God can use you. He has work for you to do and there's a special place in His plans for your unique personality. God has so much love to give to the world, but He can't simply pour it out by the bucketful. Love has to reach the heart before it can do any good in the world, and so God has to use people to distribute His love throughout the world.

By giving your life to God, you open your heart to His love and you become a new person. You become more loving, more beautiful, more like Christ, and your life has a meaning. Your best qualities just naturally seem to take over your personality and you really feel at home with yourself. This isn't the kind of happiness you can keep to yourself, and so you begin to share it. You give others some of the love God has given you—and this is how you become a beautiful person.

Jesus is the answer to the restlessness many young people feel. Don't put Him off until some other time in your life. *You need Him now!* He can show you how to be a good Christian. He can teach you how to pray with more than words so that you can really talk to God. And you *must* talk to Him if you want to discover what He wants you to do.

I believe that Jesus is the Way young people have been looking for; He is the Truth they need; He is the Life Eternal.

14

Health—Your Best Beauty Aid

🌹 *What do you*

do when you sit in front of your mirror? Do you tear yourself apart? So many girls do, and this is the worst mistake they can make!

It's a good thing God doesn't look at us as we look at ourselves! But He doesn't go along with the world's standards—He has some of His own and He can see the beauty in everyone.

If you reduce beauty to a matter of features and dimensions, no wonder you make faces at yourself! There would never be a Miss America (or a Miss Anything-Else) if beauty meant perfect features, and I would be the first to declare myself out of the running. I can point to my shortcomings, too, you know, and people are often surprised when I do. But I don't have perfect features, and I'm not perfect in any other way, either.

The time has come for all girls to stop picking on themselves. What you consider to be faults may be valuable personality traits just waiting to be used. As long as you isolate your characteristics, one from the other, they're never going to add up to the lovely person God has put together inside you.

People should be able to look at you and see the remarkable

young woman God made. Anybody can put together a man-
nequin with regular features, but only God could make you.
So, if your nose has a bump in it, be proud of it! It's the only
one of its kind.

God gave you a body to live in while you're here in this
world. It's a good body and it will perform well if you take
care of it. But if you abuse it, it will no longer reflect the
beautiful radiance inside you.

There is so much for you to do in your young years. You
need all the energy you can get and you can't afford to waste
a bit. Why should you miss out on life because you're tired?
Some girls do. They're tired all the time because they're
ignoring a few sensible rules for good health.

It isn't hard to get enough energy for ordinary daily life.
But what about those big moments? Will you be ready to do
your best and look your best for them? Or will you fall short
of your goal because you're nodding your head at the crucial
moment?

You don't have to sleep around the clock to get the rest you
need. Everybody has different requirements and you have to
discover your own, but you should try to be consistent. Get
in the habit of going to bed at a regular time every night. Naturally, there will be some exceptions—especially when those
big moments come along—but you'll be ready for them.

A girl who becomes Miss America needs the kind of stamina
that comes from years of healthy living. Otherwise she could
never finish her reign with her eyes wide open. One of the
highlights of my reign was a trip to Japan for a showing of
American fashions. I was excited about the trip and during
my two weeks in Japan I saw more than most tourists ever see.
I was on the go every minute and when I went to bed I didn't
sleep as well as usual. If I hadn't had the proper amount of
sleep for several weeks before my trip, I would have represented a pretty sluggish American girl.

Eating is another one of those ordinary things that shouldn't
be a problem in your life. If you eat too much, cut down on

the size of your meals, but don't stop eating. You need that food, and you might need more varieties of it. Be daring and try new foods, especially those green things you keep pushing over to the side of your plate.

I don't like crash diets—they live up to their name and they can do a lot of damage. Maybe I'm a coward, but I prefer to lose my pounds more slowly. It's better than being too feeble to stand on the scale!

Most teen-agers don't have to be encouraged to exercise, but when you cross over into the ancient year of twenty, you may not have as much time to get outdoors for some action. Water skiing is my favorite sport. There's something about the combination of sun, wind, and water that relaxes me completely—but I haven't been able to do much of it lately. I had to find a substitute and so I learned how to do simple indoor exercises. At least they kept me from creaking in the knees when I stooped down to talk to a little girl.

When you're under pressure, you can become a victim of tension, and that's the end of all your best efforts. Tension will never be fun, but you can learn to live with it without getting tied up in knots. If you can understand that a certain amount of tension is a natural part of any big achievement, you won't get angry about it—and anger is the thing that curls your toes. Some of the best things I've ever done have been brought out of me by the tension of trying to excel—and I wouldn't want to avoid that feeling for anything!

You can get a break from tension if it becomes too severe. Try a change of scene, or even a change of subject. Go for a short ride, take a swim or a walk, read a book—and you'll feel refreshed.

Let's face it—eating and exercise and tension aren't the biggest health problems in a young person's life. The tough ones involve drinking and smoking. I'll have to speak for myself here—and I can't very well speak for anyone else, can I?

I don't drink or smoke. I never have and I never will. My

reason is quite simple: ". . . your body is the temple of the Holy Ghost [Spirit] . . ." (I Corinthians 6:19, KJV). My body does not belong to me. It is God's and it shelters His Spirit which came to live in me when I committed my life to Him. This is the spiritual part of my life—this is where I really live.

I have no right to harm anything that belongs to God, and I believe that His Spirit needs a healthy temple. Liquor and cigarettes just don't fit in with my faith, and so they have no place in my life.

If you want a scientific argument as well, turn to the abundant proof that smoking and drinking are harmful to health. They are habits that are hard to break, and I wish young people would realize this before they get started on them. Again, it's a simple "should" that becomes complicated only when you try to get around it.

I've often been asked for my views on drinking and smoking, and I've never hesitated to give them, but someone always says, "Well, everybody else is doing it—how can a girl avoid it?" That's a loaded question. You don't have to do what everyone else is doing. You came into this world as an individual and you ought to hold onto that status. Be sure, too, that your outlook isn't colored by your temptations. Is *everybody* else drinking and smoking? Not one of my close friends does, and neither do a great many of the young people I've met —in all parts of the country. Of course, if you're looking for an excuse, you can always find one!

Yes, you'll meet some people who will coax you to try a drink or a cigarette, and you may decide that "there's no harm in just one." But hold on there a minute! That "one" is loaded with danger because it makes you give up your convictions. Whose life are you living?—yours or somebody else's? By "trying" a drink or a cigarette to find out whether you like it, you miss the whole point. Liking or not liking is *not* the question! We don't go through life doing only what we like to do and avoiding what displeases us. We do what we believe is right, and we avoid, with God's help, the wrong things. I believe that smoking and drinking are wrong, and so I avoid them—and that brings me back to where I started.

Did you know that Miss America is not permitted to drink or smoke? She's not permitted to attend cocktail parties or go to nightclubs or bars or have any alcoholic beverages served at her table. Apparently lots of people think these things don't belong in the life of the American girl.

I know another question that keeps popping up at this point, and again it opens the door to a good excuse, if that's what you want. "But how do you say 'no' when someone offers you a drink?"

If you're worried about being a square, or if you think you have to drink and smoke to be popular, then you're already in trouble. You haven't used your principles often enough to develop their muscles. "No" isn't hard to say when you know why you're saying it. If you intend to take good care of the life God gave you, you can even afford to smile when you say "no." Don't be sheepish about taking a stand on your faith. You may offend the crowd, that's true, but would you rather offend God?

What's your health worth to you? Is it worth being a square? Is it worth the realization that you didn't make a fool of yourself at a party? Would you rather ask your friends to tell you what happened after you blacked out? Would you rather give up those long swims because your lung power isn't what it used to be?

Take a look at the "rounds." They can't be having such a good time if they keep trying to get away from it all. Why are they running away from life? Healthy habits give you the ability to taste life's finest flavors. Is this what you want to give up?

A girl who makes the most of the gifts God gave her is an outgoing, vigorous person who never has to wonder what to do next. So many things are happening in her life and she doesn't want to miss a single minute of the excitement. The

92

years that stretch out ahead of her look good to her. She wants all her memories to be absolutely clear. This is a girl you can't miss. She's a knockout because she gives herself the best beauty care in the world—a healthy way of life.

15

Facing the World

❧ *When I talk*
about makeup, I feel like such an amateur. I don't know very
much about the subject—in fact, I don't even use much makeup.
If this surprises you, you're not the only one. A woman who
was interviewing me during a radio broadcast suddenly inter-
rupted our conversation and said, almost accusingly, "You're an
attractive girl—yet you don't wear any of that junk the kids
wear today." Well, she was wrong, but she paid me a very fine
compliment. I was wearing my usual makeup, and I told her
so, but I'm not sure she believed me. You see, my makeup
didn't "show," and that's how I knew I had applied it correctly.

Makeup might be considered a form of art, and I go along
with William Shakespeare who said that art should "hold the
mirror up to nature." But this isn't what the cosmetics ads have
in mind. They seem to encourage girls to hold a blanket up to
nature.

One of the most beautiful things about the human face is its
ability to reflect a person's innermost feelings through expres-
sions. This is a vital line of communication between your
inner self and the outside world, and the line should be kept
clear and flexible. Too much makeup can freeze your face
into a mask that says nothing. If you use makeup, don't be
heavy-handed. I know how pretty all those tubes and bottles
and brushes look on the cosmetics counters, but let them stay
there.

If you see a pretty face on a magazine cover—watch out! It's not for you! Actresses and models work under harsh, bright lights that rob their faces of all natural color, and so they have to compensate by overdoing their makeup. If you were to copy their techniques, you might look more like a clown than a girl in the softer light of your daily life. You must also remember that the girl on the magazine cover is supposed to sell the magazine, and that means she has to stand out among a lot of other attractive girls on magazine covers. She may do it by using some far-out makeup techniques.

You want to stand out, too, don't you? That's all right—it's part of being a girl—but you should stand out by being your radiant self and not a freak.

The right amount of makeup will highlight your best features, never exaggerate them. This is the kind you can wear comfortably, without that awful feeling that people are staring at you. Let the fashions come and go—the natural look is always "in."

Makeup isn't a substitute for good grooming. It won't hide a skin that isn't scrubbed or hair that isn't brushed. If you want to look your best, you have to polish your features, not change them. You shouldn't ever be too tired to shampoo your hair once or twice a week, and cleaning your nails and brushing your teeth don't require much energy. When these little grooming habits become as natural as breathing, you'll feel the way you look—lovely!

Glamour can be a girl's worst enemy if it costs her her individuality. If you're trying to be glamorous today, you're probably wearing a large mouth, sinister eyes, and rash-pink skin. You also look like a million other girls—is that so great?

I was very tempted to try to look glamorous when I became Miss America. It's quite an experience to sit down before a whole tray full of cosmetics, and I must admit I tried a few that I wouldn't ordinarily have used. I even wore false eyelashes for some of my stage appearances—and let me tell you, they're quite uncomfortable! When I saw some of my new photographs, something seemed to be missing, but I couldn't be sure what it was.

Then, one day, when I was sitting backstage before doing a performance, a little girl came up to say "hello" to me. That always brought a lump to my throat because I remembered how I looked up to Miss America when I was a little girl, and I wanted to be worthy of this highest form of admiration. My tiny fan watched me very closely as we chatted, and I was so happy when I realized that I had forgotten to wear my false eyelashes! Miss America has to be absolutely real to little girls —right down to her eyelashes—and I hadn't disappointed my fan. Someday, perhaps, when her friends would urge her to be glamorous by wearing false eyelashes, she might say to herself, "Miss America didn't wear them, so I guess I can do without them, too."

Ever since that day, I've remembered to forget to wear my fake eyelashes. I also began to eliminate some other new cosmetics I had tried, and I began to feel like myself again. I could even see the difference in the next set of photographs—I recognized myself.

You'll always seem like a stranger to yourself when you follow the latest fads in fashion. You won't be comfortable with anything less than your own style, your own look, and you can find it only by following the line of your own features.

Choose your own makeup foundation—cream or powder— but choose a color that belongs to your skin. If you want to brighten up your face, use just a bit of something pink on your cheekbones—but so lightly that you can hardly see it.

Eyes take a lot of punishment from makeup these days, and sometimes they can't be seen behind all the frills that are supposed to enlarge them. Your eyelids are fine, exactly as they are. You can't ever convince me that they ought to be blue or green or any other color. And eye shadow won't do anything for your eyes except call attention away from them—which isn't the effect you're trying to achieve!

You may not need anything on your eyebrows, either. If they are very thin, you might try filling in here and there with a pencil, but use a color that matches your hair. If they complement your eyes as they are, let them be or you'll ruin your expression. I use a few strokes of an eyebrow pencil to blend in a scar over my right eyebrow, but I wouldn't even do that if it made me look artificial.

I guess I'm not much help on makeup because, frankly, I've always preferred to get along with a minimum amount of it. I want to look as attractive as possible, and I don't think that's necessarily a sign of vanity—although I think it's feminine. I just don't consider makeup attractive if it looks obvious.

I know what I like to see when I look in my mirror, but you'll have to suit yourself as far as your appearance is concerned. I like to recognize myself. I don't like to see colors that don't look like the ones God gave me. My brown hair may be a fairly common shade that I see on many other girls, but God must like it or He wouldn't have given it to me. I don't want to change the shape of the features He gave me, either, but I don't think I'm wrong to want them to look their very best.

I choose my makeup with these things in mind, and I'm afraid I don't pay much attention to fads or fashions. I use a cream foundation because it looks like the skin it covers. I like to use an eye liner, too, but only in shades of charcoal or brown —black is much too harsh. I don't really care for eye shadow because it gives my eyes a hard, unnatural look. I wear my hair long because I like to change the style now and then, and you can't do that with short hair. And whether my hair is up or down, it's always brushed until it gets that special shine.

A fancy hairstyle for a special evening event can give a girl a great boost, but you can't live with that sort of thing every day. I'm more comfortable in a casual style that I can manage in case I don't have time to go to the hairdresser—which is almost always. I'm afraid, too, that I'm one of those girls who is able to sleep on a head full of rollers, but I wouldn't dream of wearing them anywhere—even under a scarf—in public. For that matter, they aren't nice to see around the house, either!

Miss America is a fashionable young woman with a $10,000 wardrobe designed just for her. This is a delightful experience, and it really makes a girl think carefully about the clothes she chooses to wear. I always try to wear clothes that flatter me, but I don't go overboard for the fashion trends that come and go so fast. I choose my clothes to last, and they have to be able to go everywhere, so I prefer the simple styles that are always attractive.

Hats are things I learned to wear by being Miss America, and I must say that I had a lot of fun with them. They keep a girl's hair in place, too. Of course, I had a wonderful experience—I didn't have to pay for my hats. They were gifts, and all I had to do was like them and wear them—and who wouldn't? I come from the West, where people live very casually, and I hardly ever wore a hat back home. I used to sing in the church choir, so I didn't even wear a hat on Sundays. In the East you see many more hats—in fact, Eastern women generally dress more formally, and I don't know which tradition I prefer. I guess I like both, depending upon the occasion. It's comfortable to wear sports clothes when you're very active, but it's nice to get dressed up for a special event.

Gloves are a must for me, and although I always feel "right" with white ones, I sometimes like to wear gloves that match my purse. Whatever the color, I don't feel like a lady without them.

A dress that fits you will look better than a dress that fits the latest fashion. I know I'm open to criticism in this department, but I can't feel comfortable in a dress that is too tight, too loose, too short, or too long—and if I'm not comfortable I can't look well in anything. It's good to be aware of your shortcomings so that you won't pick colors or styles that emphasize them, but you can go too far in this direction. If you're a fault-finding person, nothing will please you.

Every girl likes to wear skirts and blouses, but two-piece out-fits really look better on tall girls. This doesn't mean you have to stick to one-piece dresses if you're 5'2" or under. You may look your best in a dress, but you can get away with a skirt and blouse as long as the blouse is tucked in the skirt and the skirt has straight lines. Don't envy the tall girl, either, be-cause she has problems of her own. She doesn't look well in stripes and she may be crazy about them!

The heels of shoes are going up and down as much as the hemlines of dresses, but I can't get around in those spike heels, no matter how popular they may be. I like a medium heel that lets me walk without feeling that I'm going to fall.

Taste is something that varies from girl to girl, but no girl can be attractive in clothes that aren't kept neat and fresh. You may joke about your messy clothes closet that spills over into your room every time you open the door, but people won't joke about you if you're a messy girl. You can't simply buy clothes —you have to take care of them. They weren't made to be thrown on the floor or piled on chairs. They were made for hangers, drawers, and shelves, and that's where you should keep them.

Laundries are everywhere, too, and you have time to use them. I don't care who designed your lovely dress—if it's full of wrinkles, you'll be runner-up to the girl in the freshly laun-dered skirt and blouse.

Your appearance is important and you should care about the impression you give to people. It's their introduction to you, and if they like what they see, they'll want to know you better. You can't always present your whole personality and character in one brief moment, so you have to rely on your appearance to give people a preview of the person you really are.

Don't sell people short by masquerading as someone else. The worst part about such a deception is that it usually portrays you as someone who can't hold a candle to the real you.

16

Live Up to Your Looks

❧ *A girl doesn't*
become Miss America simply by performing well onstage.
From the moment the contestants arrive in Atlantic City
for the National Finals until a few moments before the crown
is placed on the head of one of them, their behavior is scrutinized. Offstage and on, relaxed or tensed for a big moment,
they are judged.

There's a good reason for this. Miss America will meet a
lot of people and the Pageant officials want to be sure that she
will live up to her title. They don't want the American girl
to be represented by someone who merely looks the part.
They want someone who can make people feel that they've
known her a long time. She has to feel comfortable with people.

Each evening during the week of the Finals, each contestant
must dress in a formal gown and have dinner in the dining
room of her hotel. She is accompanied by her chaperone and
no one else, not even a member of her family. This is a bit of a
strain, but that's part of the test. A girl with real poise never
lets people down.

Do you live up to people's expectations? Do you dress taste-
fully, make up your face carefully, and then just stand there
waiting for the world to fall at your feet? Then it isn't surprising that people pass you by. You've bottlenecked your
beauty!

Beauty needs many means of expression, and no girl can afford to ignore such things as grace, charm, and poise. I know how many rules are being thrown aside these days, but let's hold onto these!

Yes, you *should* do something about the way you walk if it portrays you as a clumsy young woman—and you're not. Then why not learn to walk more gracefully? You don't have to do anything elaborate, but an improvement in your posture would surely help. You walk around with your head down— is that the way you feel about life?

Good posture doesn't make you as stiff as a board, so relax. You can't look your best when your arms hang rigidly at your sides. If you can't talk yourself into relaxation, try a few exercises. Bend your head down and swing it slowly from side to side until you begin to feel those neck muscles loosening up. If you need more, bend over from the waist and let your arms hang loose—then shake them as if you were a rag doll. The best exercise is probably the easiest—just yawn. You may feel a bit silly when you do these things, but you'll welcome the improvement in your disposition. They're especially helpful when you're tense from studying for that big exam.

Conversation is a big problem for some girls and it shouldn't be. There isn't any mystery to the "good conversationalist"—she usually knows better than to let the whole burden fall on her shoulders. If you feel that you have to do all the talking, naturally you'll run out of subject matter. But if you ask a few questions, you can learn something about the other side of conversation—listening.

Don't listen only with your ears. Use your eyes, your whole face, to let the other person know that her words are important to you. Have you ever spoken to someone who stares back at you with a glazed look in her eyes? Well, remember that, and don't ever duplicate it!

When I was in Atlantic City for the Pageant, a reporter glanced at my dummy and said, "You're the first ventriloquist I've ever seen in the Miss America Pageant, and I've watched them for twelve years." "Twelve years!" I said— "You must have seen some wonderful girls and some wonderful talents!" Well, I thought he would never stop talking! He told me all about every contestant he had ever seen and I found it very interesting. When we said "good-bye," he called me "a good conversationalist" but he hadn't written down a word I said!

That experience confirmed something I was beginning to understand. I used to give a lot of thought to the things I planned to say to people. Now I know that it's more important to find out what's on their minds.

If you can bring out someone else's personality, you'll both be more at ease, and you'll probably begin to talk at the same time. You may have heard people say that you have to have confidence in yourself, but that's a big order. Someone else has to have confidence in you, first. If you have poise, you'll be aware that you're not the only person in the world, and you'll want to give some assurance to others.

It's nice to be able to think of things to say, but what good are they if you mumble your words? You can't blame people for being shocked when a lovely girl walks up to them with a graceful step and opens her mouth to release a long string of words that literally bump into each other. Perhaps she's a brilliant girl, but who can tell?

So few girls pay attention to the tone of their voice, yet a pleasant speaking voice can be an expression of beauty. A flat, nasal, or harsh voice can make a listener close his mind, if not his ears, but a soft, steady, musical voice gets an immediate audience. It's worth your time to practice some of the speech exercises you can find in any good book on the subject. Use a tape recorder, too, if you can get your hands on one. Nothing can teach you faster than the sound of your own mistakes, and each improvement will give you tremendous encouragement.

I enjoy performing on a stage, but I realize that it isn't fun for everyone. Still, any girl might find herself up on a platform, even though she never goes near a theater, and she ought to be prepared for it.

If you ever have to speak to your church group, to your women's club, to a scout meeting, a civic group, or any one of the many other gatherings that may call upon you some day, think about the people sitting in the last row. It's natural for an inexperienced speaker to fasten her eyes on the people sitting right in front of her, and if this happens to you, your voice will never get beyond the range of your eyes. By the time your words come to an end, you'll probably be whispering and your message will be lost to all but a few.

Pay more attention to that back row! You don't have to stare at the people, but let them hear what you have to say. This is known as "throwing" your voice. It takes a lot of practice and it really brings you out of your shell. After all, you can't behave like a mouse if you don't sound like one any more!

As long as you're putting so much time and effort into your speaking ability, you might as well put yourself to the test. If you haven't been an active member of any group, now is the time to get moving. Join a group, if you don't belong to one, and speak your mind if you're already a member. A girl like you shouldn't sit on life's sidelines. You ought to be in there where things are going on.

What's the real meaning of all these improvements you've been making? They're nice to have, aren't they, but what are you going to do with them? Specifically, what are you going to do with *you?*

By now you should begin to realize how many blessings you have. You're a beautiful girl, you have many talents, you like people, and they like you. You have a mind, too, and some of your thoughts are pretty interesting, aren't they? In fact, they often surprise you!

Having so much isn't enough, though. You want to do something with all your blessings; you want to invest them in the world, in people. How? You want to do the right things

103

and make the right kind of investments so that you don't squander your blessings foolishly.

This isn't a simple problem and you won't find a simple answer. It calls for serious thinking and all the help you can get.

17

Is Your Goal Big Enough?

❧ *I was no* sooner chosen Miss America when people began asking me what I planned to do when my reign was over. It was hard enough to think about the next year without worrying about the one after it, but I realized that the questions were perfectly normal. They weren't so different from the ones I had heard since I was a little girl—"What are you going to be when you grow up?" I guess we've all heard that one enough times.

Are you able to answer it yet? You can give some pretty fantastic answers when you're very young, or you can shrug it off and go play with your dolls, but it can really begin to bother you as you get older. Even your school begins to needle you about it, and you find yourself taking test after test. But why?

You may have a hard time making up your mind about the direction your future is going to take, but you can't be vague forever. These are your best years of preparation and you could be investing them in your career—if only you knew what it was going to be.

Okay, don't put a label on your future yet—there's still time to settle the final details. But you can begin to sample the experience of going after something you want. You're hardly too young for that and you've probably been doing it without realizing it.

Perhaps you have gone through something as laborious as

practicing the scales on a piano, or a violin, or some other musical instrument. Hardly anyone can call that a joy, but when you play your first piece of music all the way through you begin to understand what those hours of practice meant. And they were worthwhile, weren't they? You reached your goal!

If you're interested in sports, you've had good training in heading toward a goal. You know what it is to practice, to get better and better and closer and closer to that goal, and you've probably had the satisfaction of reaching it.

The fortunate things that drop into your lap are great, but they can't give you the feeling of achievement that comes with striving for something very important. That's why you have to think about your future and make up your mind about it. You have to work your way into it, and that takes plenty of time and effort.

You're a talented girl, so don't waste your abilities on a goal that won't make demands on you. Little goals give little satisfaction. You need something big in your future, something that will use every gift you have, and even show you some undiscovered ones!

If your goal is a good one, remember that other people are going to want it, too, and you'll face some stiff competition. Does that make you want to change your mind? It shouldn't. If lots of people want the same thing, there may be something to it.

I was a senior in high school when I thought it might be nice to compete in The America's Junior Miss Pageant. The winner represents the ideal high-school girl, and special emphasis is placed on talent, character, high-school activities, personal ambitions, citizenship, poise, and demeanor. I guess I really wanted to find out whether I had those qualities and in what degree, but ten thousand other girls felt the same way! That's how many contestants made up my competition throughout the country, and I began to have second thoughts. It's one thing to compete in the preliminary contests in your own hometown, but when you realize that thousands of girls are doing the same thing in hundreds of hometowns, you get pretty scared!

It's a good thing my mother doesn't scare as easily as I do. When I told her that I didn't think I had a chance to do anything more than make a fool of myself in the contest, she said, "Vonda, you have just as good a chance as any other girl." She was so matter-of-fact about it! And she was absolutely right!

I took Kurley along with me because an important part of the contest was the talent competition. Our performance was a new experience for us. We weren't only trying to entertain the audience—we were trying to entertain them better than any of the other contestants could. We were out to win a prize, plus a chance to become Arizona's Junior Miss for 1961.

I found that I liked competition. I was in very good company and I made some new friends. People may tell you that competition is ruthless, but that isn't the way it was for me. The other girls in the contest were having fun, just as I was, and we all had such an enthusiastic audience. We couldn't help but want to do our best.

Performing before an audience has always given me a special pleasure. It gives me an opportunity to share my talents with other people, and this is a way of saying, "Thank you, God, for all You've given me." When a girl can perform in a contest and hope to get an award for doing it, she has a double opportunity.

It's wonderful to perform when part of your audience is your competition. They know, more than any of the others, how much hard work went into your accomplishments, and you'll find respect as well as encouragement in their applause.

It's hard to avoid some form of competition in life. It stands between you and anything worthwhile, and it's there for a good reason. As long as you develop your talents to suit you, your family, your friends, and your immediate neighborhood, you're never going to experience that final push, that maximum effort, that big stretch that turns an aim into an achievement. You're capable of so much more than you realize, but something else will have to bring your most amazing qualities out into the open. You need a goal, you need something far more important than your own satisfaction. A goal that's worthy of you will make you grow.

Don't say you aren't ready to aim for something you want. How do you know you aren't ready? You can't rely on your own judgment—you're too close to your faults. The only way you can find out how far you've come and how far you have to go is to get out and compare yourself with the rest of the world.

I used to think of Kurley as a nice little hobby until I used him in my first pageant. Maybe I had treated him as a doll, but nobody else did! I couldn't always tell how well I was doing when I performed for my friends—maybe they were only being kind. I knew the Pageant audience and the judges would be far more objective, and I was eager to get their opinion. I was flabbergasted! I won! And I kept on winning.

I can't say that my work with a dummy was actually hard, but I gave it a lot of my time and most of my determination. I thought I owed that much to any ability God saw fit to give me. Now I realized that something new was happening to my talent. For one thing, I was sharing it with many more people, which was certainly a pleasure for me. Still, I couldn't help feeling that a much more important experience was going to come out of it. I'd have to wait and see where it was going to take me.

18

Learn How to Lose

❧ *I'll never say*

that losing doesn't matter. Of course it does. It hurts and it shakes your confidence in yourself—but the damage shouldn't be permanent.

Whenever you try to win something, you have to face the possibility that you might fail to get it. Sometimes there's only one prize to go around and only one girl can win it. Does that mean the other hopefuls are losers? No, indeed.

You can lose only if you quit, if you give up trying. I've seen some quitters in beauty pageants and every one of them could have been a winner if she had had one of the most vital qualifications for success—persistence. Winning isn't something you can do with a snap of the fingers, or even overnight, regardless of the stories publicity men dream up. Winning takes a long time, and winners are people who go all the way to their goals, no matter how many times they have to take a step backward and start over. If you've ever been in a competition, you'll sense this quality in any contestants who've been through it more than once.

How do you feel about losing? Would it make you feel ashamed? Now, that's where you're so wrong! You can learn how to win by losing, because losing is an excellent teacher.

When I went to the Junior Miss National Finals in Mobile, Alabama, my hopes were very high. Although I really hadn't expected to get as far as the state title, I couldn't help wondering how it would be to go all the way to the top. But a different kind of experience awaited me.

I got as far as the top ten, and I had a chance to win. I could feel myself stiffening with tension as we entered the final round of competition, and that was something new to me. My performance wasn't quite the way it usually was, but I didn't know what was wrong. Whatever it was, it affected my timing.

I was up against nine highly accomplished high-school girls and I had to admit that they were all potential winners. If they were as nervous as I was, they didn't show it. And when one of them was named America's Junior Miss, the others seemed to be so happy for her. I smiled and applauded as hard as I could and hoped I was covering up my disappointment as well as they were. Surely they must have felt crushed!

Losing gives you a sinking sensation, no matter how much you try to prepare for it. It cuts your ambition off at its peak, and there seems to be nothing ahead of you. Suddenly the busy whirl of the days and weeks and months comes to a stop, and you wonder what to do with yourself. Even packing is a dreary business that can be done in a few moments—and just think how long it took you to do it only a week ago! Everything had to be carefully folded then—now you don't care whether your clothes get wrinkled.

If you've ever felt like this, then you won't get my sympathy. I gave it all to myself a long time ago, and it was the worst thing I could have done. When you lose, or when you fail to reach your goal, you shouldn't take time out to weep about it. You've got so much work to do. You see, you've just taken inventory of yourself.

When you lose, there's a reason for it. Either you don't have what it takes or you aren't using what you've got. Either way, you'll have to make some improvements in yourself. Suppose you ran for class president and lost the election. Does that mean that you don't have a future in politics? No, ma'am! You weren't good enough and you've got to do better next

110

time! Don't waste your time talking about the luck you didn't have. *Nobody ever has any luck,* because there's no such thing. Winners earn their rewards.

Losing one pageant didn't make me want to stop competing, but I didn't learn anything from it, either. I simply thought I might have a better chance in another contest, and I set my sights on the Miss Phoenix Pageant the next year. That was the local competition that began the search for Miss America, a very important goal for me.

Only one thing was different in that contest. I was even more nervous and I didn't do as well as usual. I lost because I deserved to lose, but that only made me angry with myself.

I've never been short on determination and again I tried to win the title of Miss Phoenix during my sophomore year in college. I certainly tried hard, and my efforts got me as far as first runner-up, but I didn't even feel like myself. I was so tense that I raced through my act with Kurley and eliminated some of my best jokes along the way—I guess I wanted to get off that stage in a hurry!

That did it! I was through with pageants or any other kind of competition. I didn't have enough talent, or enough poise, or whatever else I needed. I didn't have anything! How foolish I must have looked!

It was time for me to begin my junior year at Arizona State University and I welcomed a change of subject as well as scene. I didn't have to go far from home—the University was in nearby Tempe, in the same county—and that was good because I needed the comfort and assurance of my family.

I had hoped to forget about the contests, but I couldn't. Something kept bothering me. The disappointments had vanished long ago—what else was left? I was about to find out.

I had plunged into my studies with a special eagerness but another educational process was going on in my spirit. I began to understand why I had lost. First of all, I hadn't done my best. Oh, I had tried hard, but that wasn't the same as doing my best.

111

I was aiming for the wrong goal and for the wrong reasons. The prize was the only thing I could see. I didn't really appreciate the competition or the opportunity it offered me. I had to have it and I wanted it all for myself. I had never even asked myself whether I was doing the right thing—and I had never asked God how He felt about it. That would have been easy. Christ has always walked close beside me and I could have asked Him what God thought I should have done.

No, I had to go off on my own and make all the decisions! Well, I had done a beautiful job of it. Straight F's, all the way! I certainly wouldn't do anything like that again!

Of course, my friends didn't know what I was thinking. They knew I hadn't performed well and they wanted me to have another chance to win the state title. They wanted me to enter the Miss Tempe contest, since my residence at ASU now made me eligible for it.

"Not on your life!" I said. I wasn't going to make another decision on my own! I knew exactly what I had to do with my life.

Did I? How did I know? Had I asked my Friend what He thought of the Tempe Pageant? I had done it again, in spite of all my promises—I had made my own decision. After all, "no" is just as much a decision as "yes," isn't it?

There was only one thing to do. I prayed. I asked God to guide me in making a decision. I knew what *I* wanted to do, but that didn't matter. I would do whatever *God* wanted me to do.

He wanted me to enter the contest, and that just shows you how much I knew about running my life. That wasn't the decision I would have made and I was very honest about it. "All right," I said, when I felt that my prayers were answered, "I lost when I did things my way. Now we'll try Your way— but I don't see what difference that's going to make. If I'm not good enough, I'm not good enough."

God's way *was* different, and I noticed the change immediately. I realized that I needed much more practice as a ven-

112

triloquist, and practice of a kind I had never had. My act needed the professional polish that comes from professional experience. I didn't have to wonder where I was going to get that experience—I knew.

A family fun park named Legend City was opening near Phoenix and it was just the place for Kurley and me. The front half of the park was a careful duplication of a typical frontier town of the Old West—complete with gold mine, jail, general store, stable, wooden sidewalks—and a jaunty showboat tied up along the shore by the canal. A Music Hall offered soft drinks, snacks, and excellent entertainment by young professional performers, and it had quickly become a favorite with local young people. The management was auditioning college students, so that's where I headed.

Kurley and I auditioned and we got a job at the Music Hall, so I had to budget my time carefully. I didn't want my weekend work to interfere with my education. I was a very busy girl that year but I enjoyed every minute of it. I did several shows a day at the Legend City Music Hall and I could feel my act improving with each one of them. During the summer I stayed on and worked full time—I was really a professional! I was performing before an audience who paid admission to see professional entertainment and they wouldn't make excuses for anyone who couldn't meet their standards. When I was able to win their applause, I knew I was earning far more than a salary for my efforts.

The biggest change that came over me was my attitude toward the pageant itself. I no longer doubted that it was the right goal for me, but I knew that the first prize wasn't the only thing it offered me. I was going to do my best—and even better than that—but I wasn't going to do it in order to win a title. I was going to try to please God by making the most of a good opportunity to share my talents.

I had a new purpose in competing. I was going into that pageant to entertain the people who would be watching it, to offer them a part of all that had been given to me, and I knew that I was going to have a wonderful time. No more tension, no more straining to reach a goal that was too far away from me. Yes, one of these days I might be able to reach it, if I kept on improving myself, and in the meantime I had so much to see and do along the way. Maybe I would find the opportunity that meant more to me than any of the others—it could happen during a beauty pageant as well as anywhere else on this earth. I just might be given a chance to share the most important gift of my life—my faith in God.

19

Enjoy Yourself!

❧ *You'll never know*
how well you can do something until you begin to enjoy doing
it. When people tell you to "relax and enjoy yourself," they're
not out of their minds—they're giving you valuable advice.

When you enjoy your own talents, you release your whole
personality. You forget about such things as awards, prizes, or
special honors, and you lose yourself in the pleasure of demon-
strating something you have learned to do very well. This is
your way of telling God that you *have* counted your blessings
and you want to increase them by giving them away.

The Miss Tempe title became mine in 1964, and I went on to
the county contest. I'll never forget the feeling of warmth
and friendliness that came to me from the audience when I got
out on the stage in the Miss Maricopa Pageant. I know now
that the response had always been there, but I had been too
nervous to accept anything the audience could give me. I was
so worried about making an impression that I didn't allow the
audience to impress me with their kindness. Funny, how you
miss the best parts of human nature when you're all wound up
in yourself.

I won that contest, but I had also performed better. I was
having such a good time and I simply had to share it with my
audience. God was right—there isn't any award in the world
that can equal the satisfaction of doing your best. I didn't have
any more doubts about doing things His way.

There were more pageants ahead of me and I decided that I was going to enjoy all of them. By the time I won the county title and went on to become Miss Arizona, I forgot how it felt to be nervous. I was meeting more and more wonderful people and performing for larger and larger audiences. This was an experience I never could have had as Vonda Kay Van Dyke, coed.

Then I began to see how God could use my accomplishment. While I was Miss Arizona, I appeared on a nationwide telecast of a Billy Graham Crusade in San Diego, I had what I really wanted—a chance to talk about my faith to the largest number of people I could possibly imagine!

I was so thrilled by my Crusade experience that I couldn't possibly get nervous about the Miss America Pageant. Before I realized it, I was caught up in a week of final competitions that brought me face to face with the most talented contestants I had ever seen. By the end of the week I found myself with another appointment with a television audience—I was in the top ten again, even though I hadn't won any of the preliminary competitions during the week!

"You certainly had a ball, Vonda," my father observed after the Pageant, and he was quite right. I never thought my light-heartedness could last through those finals, but it seemed to increase with every challenge. Only once did I shed a few tears and that happened when I received the Miss Congeniality award. I was so touched.

This award meant more to me than any other I might have won. The judges had nothing to do with it—it was given by the contestants to a contestant, and it was a gesture of affection. My chaperone and some of my staunchest rooters weren't very happy about it, though, because it seemed to indicate that history was running against me. In forty-three years, no girl had ever won the Miss Congeniality award and the Miss America title, too.

I wondered how I would have felt about that award if the

Pageant title had meant everything to me. I would have been crushed and I don't know how I could have gone onstage for the last part of the Pageant. But I was too happy to be bothered by history. I had shared my friendship, my joy, and my talent with many people and that's what I had set out to do.

But what about the faith I wanted to share? I couldn't complain. I had had my big opportunity in San Diego. Yet I was still in the Pageant—maybe I would get another chance.

The chance came during the final moments of the Pageant and I might not have been ready for it if I had been worried about that first prize. Those last moments scream with suspense, and for some of the girls it's almost impossible to think of anything except the exciting future that just might be theirs. There were only five of us remaining in the competition, and I wouldn't have wanted to be a judge.

The last part of the Pageant is an interview, and the contestants don't have the slightest idea what kind of questions they will have to answer. They know the interview is supposed to bring out a vital part of each girl's character, but that's worse than knowing nothing.

I was sitting on the stage, surrounded by television lights and cameras and sound equipment, and a vast "live" audience stretched out in the darkness beyond the bright footlights. I could hear the slow, heavy breathing of everyone in that huge auditorium. Now and then I could feel the audience gasp, because they were going through these final moments with us. The only one who didn't make a sound was the Friend who brought me a feeling of peace and quiet right in the middle of the most anxious minutes. I was caught up in the suspense but I wasn't bothered by it—I was praying.

Maybe—maybe—I would be asked some kind of question that would let me talk about my faith in God and in Jesus the Friend who taught me how to enjoy every moment of life. I knew my hope was ridiculous, but I prayed as I have always prayed before going onstage: "Father, give me confidence and

117

help me to perform to the very best of my ability, and if there be any way that I can witness, give me the words to say. Amen."

Now it was my turn to step up to the microphone and wait for Bert Parks, the master of ceremonies, to read the question that was to reveal my character. It wasn't going to be easy—I had only a few seconds and I would have to think on my feet. Even if the right question came my way, I might not know what to say in such a short time.

I could tell from the first question that I was going to need all the help I could get. Bert Parks took a deep breath and read, "It's often been said that shy and retiring people by nature can only project their feelings through someone else." He paused —it was only a split second but I'm glad I didn't hold my breath that long—and then went on: "Is that the reason you took up ventriloquism?"

The words came. "No," I heard myself saying, "I didn't take it up because I'm shy in front of people. I've always been a ham. Ventriloquism is unusual and I enjoy it. This year, however, I've learned to speak for myself and I find I'm carrying Kurley less and less." My answer expressed a feeling deep within me, and I had never thought I would be able to put it into words.

Mr. Parks had another question. "I understand that you always carry a Bible with you as a good-luck charm. Tell us about your religion."

There it was. Now what was I going to say? I honestly didn't know. It was a double challenge, really, and it needed such a big answer. Someone Else would have to take over for me.

I opened my lips and the words came. "I do not consider my Bible a good-luck charm. It is the most important book I own. I would not describe my companionship with God as a religion, but as a faith. I believe in Him, trust in Him, and pray that even tonight His will may be done."

Everything else was blurred by my happiness and gratitude.

I had reached my most important goal and I had been given the words to speak. What more could I ask! I had lived through a beautiful experience. The Pageant would be over in a few minutes and I wanted to go on enjoying it. Soon I would be on my way back to the ASU campus where my friends were waiting for me. I hoped I had lived up to their faith in me.

The campus would have to wait, and so would my friends. The runners-up were being announced and all of a sudden there were only two girls left on the stage—and I was one of them.

I grasped the hand of the lovely girl sitting next to me and she gripped mine tightly. We had been through an exciting week together and we had become good friends—it was a strange experience to know that we would soon be separated by a title.

"The winner is Miss Arizona, Miss Vonda Kay Van Dyke!" The cheers, the applause, and the affection of the audience lifted me out of my chair. I was grateful—I never could have stood up by myself! The tears that had waited for so many days came spilling down my cheeks and I felt silly to be smiling and crying at the same time. It couldn't be! I had already won so much!

It's a long walk by yourself down that 240-foot runway lined with footlights, and I know I didn't look like a queen that night. I almost had to grope my way through my tears and I was sure I would wake up any moment. I wore a sparkling crown on my head, and although it was delicate I was conscious of its weight. I had won the prize, but it was not mine to keep. It belonged to my Friend, to Christ, who had given me the question and the words to answer it. I wanted to give my prize to Him—but what would He do with it?

20

Be a Good Winner

❧ *What happens when*

you win something important? Do you feel that you've arrived? You haven't. When you get to the top, you've got a long way to go.

If you win that election for class president, do you just sit back and take it easy? No, you don't. Now you have to tackle those problems and find out how to be a good administrator. All that striving, all those outstanding abilities, and even the achievement of your goal, were only promises of the things you could do. Now that you've won your prize, you have to *show* what you can do.

A new concern came to me the day after I was crowned Miss America. I didn't know how Miss America should act. Was she different from Vonda Kay Van Dyke?

She was, as Dr. Billy Graham pointed out to us in a visit with my parents and me the second morning after the Pageant. I wasn't simply a young woman with a faith and some principles—I was an example to a lot of other young women. That gave me an enormous responsibility. What a humbling experience! Together we knelt and prayed for God's guidance during the year ahead.

Now things began to make sense to me. God could do something with my title, after all. It was going to take me to many new places and I was going to meet many new people. They would come to see Miss America, and I could introduce them to the God who is the source of my strength.

It's true that Miss America is a leader of sorts, and she sets the standards for many young women who admire her achievement. But the leadership young people really need in their lives is something they can never find in any other human being. Young people need God, they need Christ as a constant Companion. That was what I hoped to be able to tell them. For a year I would have many opportunities to speak—and people would listen. I had to make those words count!

I couldn't always talk about my faith every time I opened my mouth. God isn't overbearing and I didn't want to represent Him that way. But lots of people had watched me on television during the Pageant and someone always asked me whether I still had my Bible with me. I always did, and those questions—some of them slightly sarcastic—gave me the floor.

At the beginning of my reign, I made up my mind that I would go on trying to please God in everything I did. I wanted to be able to say that I had done my best for Him every day. And my greatest blessing was that I was able to say those words at the end of my year as Miss America.

I had wanted to be Miss America for one reason—I wanted to tell people about the Christ I love and try to serve. If I inspired one young person to find a new life—a truly exciting and abundant life—in Christ, then there was great value in the crown I wore.

Some people cry when a good thing comes to an end, but I had begun my year by crying for three days and I couldn't very well end it the same way. Besides, I've never known any good thing that comes to an end—it simply leads on to something else that's good. When you let God lead you along the way, you just don't run into any dead-ends!

I wasn't sad about placing my crown on a new Miss America. I had lived a magnificent year and I would take its memories with me into the years ahead. Again, I had a ball during the Pageant that ended my reign and I was able to appreciate what courageous girls those other forty-nine contestants were. This time I was backstage when the winner was announced and I saw the faces of the losers—every one a champion! Oh, a few tears were shed, because queens are girls underneath their titles, but their applause was hearty and genuine. They were ready to go back to their states and fulfill their reigns as state queens, and they would do it wholeheartedly.

Near the end of the program I was scheduled to make a farewell speech that was supposed to last no more than one minute and thirty seconds. I had thought about that speech for several weeks before the Pageant, and I wrote it out many, many times. It was so hard to fit all my gratitude and happiness into those precious seconds. So many things had happened to me and I wanted to share them.

I kept crossing out extra words and finally was able to fit my message into the time limit. When I came out on the stage that night, I felt I was among friends I had know for a long time and my heart opened up to them. I wanted them to meet my Friend.

"My year as Miss America will not only be remembered by what I have taken from it, but by what I have become by it.

"This crown has offered many valuable gifts. It has sparkled with thousands of miles of travel. It has glowed with hundreds of priceless friendships, and it has reflected a bright new world of knowledge, with opportunities to grow both mentally and spiritually.

"These lasting, life-changing gifts deserve a thank-you to many wonderful people, but most of all to God for giving me an open mind and an open heart to take the gifts and use them.

"I ascended my throne last September with two statements: that my biggest responsibility was to live up to my Christian testimony, and that the Bible was the most important Book I owned. Tonight, I descend from my throne with the same thoughts and the same Scriptural promise which says: 'And we know that all things work together for good to them that love

God, to them who are the called according to his purpose'
(Romans 8:28, KJV).

"So, you see, I won't be stepping down. I'll be stepping
up—

to a new year,

a new life,

a new challenge!"